FAMILY LEARNING:
WHAT PARENTS
THINK

The Wider Benefits of Learning Papers

1 *Modelling and Measuring the Wider Benefits of Learning: A synthesis*
Tom Schuller, John Bynner, Andy Green, Louisa Blackwell,
Cathie Hammond, John Preston and Martin Gough

2 *Evaluating the Benefits of Lifelong Learning: A framework*
Ian Plewis and John Preston

3 *Learning to be Healthy*
Cathie Hammond

The Centre for Research on the Wider Benefits of Learning
Bedford Group for Lifecourse and Statistical Studies
Institute of Education
20 Bedford Way
London WC1H 0AL
020 7612 6900
website: *http://www.learningbenefits.net*
email: *info@learningbenefits.net*

The Centre for Research on the Wider Benefits of Learning is an independent research centre funded by the Department for Education and Skills. The views expressed in this work are those of the author and do not necessarily reflect the views of the Department for Education and Skills. All errors and omissions remain those of the author.

FAMILY LEARNING: WHAT PARENTS THINK

Angela J. Brassett-Grundy and Cathie Hammond

Centre for Research on the Wider Benefits of Learning
Bedford Group for Lifecourse and Statistical Studies
Institute of Education I Birkbeck College

First published in 2003 by the Institute of Education,
University of London, 20 Bedford Way, London WC1H 0AL

Over 100 years of excellence in education

© Institute of Education, University of London 2003

Angela Brassett-Grundy and Cathie Hammond assert the moral
right to be identified as the authors of this work.

British Library Cataloguing in Publication Data
A catalogue record for this publication is available from the
British Library

ISBN 0 85473 685 9

Cover and text design by Tim McPhee
Page make-up by Cambridge Photosetting Services, Cambridge
Production services by Book Production Consultants plc,
Cambridge
Printed by Wrightson

Contents

6 Discussion and recommendations 73

Acknowledgements

We would like to thank all of the parents who were willing to be interviewed as part of this research project, their teachers for allowing us to take up 'class' time for the focus group discussions, the head teachers and managers who allowed the research to be carried out within their schools and centres, and the following people for helping us to contact the parents who partici-pated: Jean (a London borough numeracy consultant), Linda (a London borough lifelong learning co-ordinator) and Musseret (member of a London borough lifelong learning team). The names of the parents and children used throughout this report have been changed to maintain anonymity.

Foreword

When asked by one of the authors how to promote family learning to other families, one parent replied, 'Talk us through it.' There can be no better way of whetting your appetite for the wealth of insights in this monograph, which indeed 'talks us through' family learning, in the words of parents themselves.

Too little attention has been paid to what parents and children themselves think of family learning. What do they understand by the term? How do they experience the activities organised for them? What helps and what hinders them in learning? How could it be organised better in the future? And why do some parents choose not to get involved? These are the kinds of questions the researchers asked when they talked with parents.

What parents say is well worth listening to, as it has the power to jolt professionals out of their comfort zones. Angela Brassett-Grundy and Cathie Hammond have listened carefully to what parents say, and in their thorough analysis they invite us to understand the world of parents who are (and those who are not) involved in family learning. The findings will be of interest to a wide range of people committed to developing and improving family learning opportunities.

This monograph can inspire us to develop the tools for talking about family learning with parents and children. It suggests ways of making meaning from what parents tell us about learning together. It shows us how we can value what counts in family learning, not simply count what is to hand.

So read and enjoy this monograph but, more important, talk about the research with the people you know and work with in family learning –

parents, colleagues, and decision-makers. In this way, the publication will make an important contribution to the community of debate in family learning.

Jeanne Haggart
Development Officer (Family Learning), NIACE

Preface

The Centre for Research on the Wider Benefits of Learning was established in 1999 by the then Department for Education and Employment, now the Department for Education and Skills (DfES). The Centre's task is to investigate the non-economic benefits that learning brings to the individual learner and to society as a whole. This is a joint initiative between the Institute of Education and Birkbeck College, University of London.

This monograph presents the findings from a qualitative research project investigating parental views of family learning, specifically what family learning might look like to parents, what their expectations of it might be, how they would want it to happen and where, what they might get out of it, and the right way of describing it from their point of view, i.e. a bottom-up approach. This has been set in the context of a review of the literature relating to family learning, which examines the scope of family learning, the importance of families in learning (a rationale for family learning), and evidence relating to the wider benefits of family learning. We hope that it helps highlight the importance and value of family learning, and, more importantly, the importance of listening to the people who engage in it.

We would like to thank our colleagues at the Centre for Research on the Wider Benefits of Learning, and Sue Stone and her colleagues at the DfES, for their helpful comments on earlier versions of this paper.

Chapter 1

Introduction

All families are potentially both supportive and rich learning environments for all family members. This is recognised in the government's white paper, *Learning to Succeed* (DfES, 1999), which states that along with community and adult learning, family learning is 'essential in the learning age'. The subject of family learning has increasingly become a popular subject for research and attempts have been made to raise its public profile through Family Learning Weekends, Adult Learners' Week and initiatives such as Sure Start.

Ofsted report that the organisation of family learning is fragmented over a number of departments and providers – many of which have short-term funding – which work to different objectives. This reflects an absence of clear policies for family learning (Ofsted, 2000: 7). *A Manifesto for Family Learning* (Campaign for Learning *et al.*, 2000), published by the Campaign for Learning in conjunction with National Institute of Adult and Continuing Education, CEDC, the Scottish Council Foundation and Education Extra, calls for strategic and co-ordinated planning and the development of clear policies. *National Mapping of Family Services in England and Wales* also highlights the need for national standardisation of all forms of parenting and family support (Henricson *et al.*, 2001).

In this context, the expansion of nationally co-ordinated family literacy programmes linked to the expansion of Sure Start proposed by the DfEE (2000) is very welcome, and so too is the toolkit for family learning practitioners, *Walking Ten Feet Tall*, recently published by NIACE and the DfES (Haggart, 2001). However, if the government, local authorities and partners/ providers are to continue to develop policies and strategies that improve the effectiveness of family learning, then these must be well informed by research. The research presented here was commissioned by the DfES. It addresses parental perceptions of wider outcomes of family learning, and of the aspects of provision thought to be most effective in generating benefits for individuals, families, communities, and society.

In this introductory section, we examine the scope of family learning. This is followed by discussion of the importance of families in learning (a rationale for family learning), and evidence relating to the wider benefits of family learning. This leads to a call for a large-scale in-depth evaluation of family learning.

THE SCOPE OF FAMILY LEARNING

In its broadest sense, family learning refers to all learning that takes place in and around families. NIACE and the Campaign for Learning use descriptions of family learning based upon one first published in *Riches Beyond Price* (Alexander and Clyne, 1995), which identifies five distinct aspects of family learning:
- informal learning within the family
- family members learning together
- learning about family roles, relationships and responsibilities (this includes parenting education)
- learning how to understand, take responsibility and make decisions in relation to wider society, in which the family is a foundation for citizenship
- learning how to deal with agencies that serve families.

The definition of family learning used in a report to the National Advisory Group for Continuing Education and Lifelong Learning further includes tackling the learning needs of individual family members, and family members learning about the same topic independently (Buffton, 1999: 12). These definitions encompass and go beyond Ofsted's report on family learning, which refers to 'learning which brings together different family members to work on a common theme for some, if not for the whole, of a planned programme' (Ofsted, 2000: 5).

Ofsted report that the most frequently encountered examples of formal family learning in England are family literacy schemes and emerging family numeracy programmes, targeted towards parents and children with basic skills needs. Ofsted also identifies a small but significant element of family learning programmes which cover a wider curriculum: arts and crafts, information and communications technology (ICT), music, cookery and language learning.

But what does family learning mean to members of families? How do they think family learning should be organised, and who do they think should be involved in family learning? These are some of the questions that this research attempts to address.

EVIDENCE THAT FAMILIES ARE IMPORTANT FOR LEARNING – THE RATIONALE FOR FAMILY LEARNING

This section examines the role of parents in determining their children's educational success, then broadens to discuss the importance of parents in relation to emotional learning and the development of citizenship. The emphasis on parents is not intended to exclude other family members, for example siblings and grandparents, but reflects a similar emphasis in research on the role of parents upon their children's development, and a focus upon parents as participants in family learning projects.

Smith and Spurling (2000), working closely with the Campaign for Learning, have examined motivation to learn within the family. They suggest that if a family shares goals and fosters a team spirit, individuals' motivations to learn are replaced by family-based motivations. This can create a 'learning buzz', which is immensely effective in motivating learning amongst all individuals in the family. Evidence that families are important in shaping young people's attitudes towards learning supports this suggestion. For example, Gorard *et al.* (1998), investigating learning trajectories over the life course, conclude that long-term learning identities are formed within families; indeed, the Campaign for Learning survey run by MORI reveals that just over two thirds of 12- to 16-year-olds rate their parents as the strongest learning influence in their lives (Campaign for Learning, 2000).

If families affect young people's attitudes towards learning, they will also affect their attainment. A longitudinal study of 76 infants suggests that parental levels of education play an important role in the cognitive development of children from as early as 12 months (Roberts *et al.*, 1999). Bynner and Steedman (1995) and Bynner, Joshi and Tsatsas *et al.* (1999) used national longitudinal datasets of cohorts born in 1958 and 1970 to analyse which variables determine educational success of schoolchildren born in Britain. They conclude that parental levels of education are critically important. Probable explanations for the finding are that education affects parenting styles and more specifically, attitudes towards learning and relationships with schools as providers of learning.

Based upon analyses of the same longitudinal dataset relating to the cohort born in 1958, Parsons and Bynner (1998) report particular aspects of parenting that appear to lead to the educational success of children. All other things being equal, children whose parents share parenting responsibilities and who read with them are more likely than other children to achieve educational success. The importance of shared educational tasks between parent and child, for example shared reading, as a predictor of educational achievement has been found elsewhere (Mortimore, 1988; Tizard *et al.*, 1988).

Several of the studies mentioned above also report evidence that the quality of the relationship between parents and schools correlates with children's attainment (Mortimore, 1988; Tizard *et al.*, 1988; Bynner and Steedman, 1995). Tizard *et al.* (1988) and Cuckle (1996) suggest that good communication between home and school may determine how effectively parents and caregivers are able to help their children. In addition, family learning based in schools and other formal providers of education can promote better communication between family members and these institutions.

Interestingly, Mortimore (1988) reports a negative correlation between the effectiveness of schools overall and the activity of parent teacher associations. This may reflect the fact that some but not all types of contact and activity reflect effective partnerships between schools and families, in which the key elements are shared understanding, goals, and mutual respect, as suggested by Edwards and Warin (1999). In addition, we should be aware that children, especially those of secondary school age, may not benefit from the involvement of their own parents in school because this involvement prevents them from keeping separate their home and school lives, and may place additional pressure upon them to perform in both settings. In other words, it can stop children from getting a break.

If parenting education, or indeed any form of learning that contributes to positive parenting, is included under the umbrella of family learning (as it is in many definitions), then this will contribute to the development in children not only of the motivation to learn throughout life and educational success, but also to the development of positive psychosocial qualities. In his influential book *Emotional Intelligence*, Daniel Goleman extols the importance of the family as a site for emotional learning:

> Family life is our first school for emotional learning; in this intimate cauldron we learn how to feel about ourselves and how others will react to our feelings.
>
> (Goleman, 1996: 189–90)

Central to emotional learning is the development of resilience – the ability to cope successfully with adverse events and stressors. Osborne analysed longitudinal data to investigate which factors predict the development of resilience amongst children, and concludes that 'non authoritarian attitudes and child-centred parenting coupled with a strong positive attitude to the child's education' (Osborne, 1990: 45) far outweigh the effects of other factors hypothesised to be important in determining resilience.

Families also have the capacity to foster qualities of citizenship. Buffton claims that:

> Family learning ... promotes active citizenship and, as the family group is the microcosm of the community, is community capacity building at its best.
>
> (Buffton, 1999: 2)

Family learning can have positive effects upon the development of qualities such as resilience and citizenship. In NIACE's most recent publication about family learning, Haggart suggests that family learning empowers families and thereby plays 'a part in tackling the inequalities that prevent individuals and families realising their potential' (Haggart, 2000: xiii).

Individuals and families who cannot achieve their potential without tackling inequalities are often the same individuals and families who are disengaged from formal learning. This brings us to an aspect of family learning that is of crucial importance, namely that family learning has the potential to engage a very wide range of parents, including those who are educationally and/or socially excluded, and disadvantaged in other ways.

Parents are highly motivated to help their children and this motivation may lead to participation in family learning programmes. Most evaluations of family learning programmes find them to be particularly effective in attracting and retaining parents from a wide range of backgrounds. Ofsted reports that models of family learning where the curriculum is broad have greater success in attracting participants from disadvantaged and under-represented groups (Ofsted, 2000: 8). Presumably, this is because a broader curriculum increases the chances that parents from diverse backgrounds find a course which interests them and which they feel confident enough to attend. In relation to these groups, family learning has the potential to change parental attitudes towards learning and break inter-generational cycles of educational disadvantage.

Family learning also has the potential to draw fathers more closely into their family units. Recent analyses of almost 8,500 adults born in 1958 suggest that fathers' involvement in family life protects the psychological health of their children as they grow up. The researchers conclude that:

> Father involvement at age 7 protected against psychological maladjust-
> ment in adolescents from non-intact families, and father involvement
> at age 16 protected against adult psychological distress in women.
>
> (Flouri and Buchanan, 2003: 63)

At present, mothers are heavily over-represented in most family learning programmes. However, a number of initiatives targeted at male carers have successfully recruited fathers, grandfathers, and other male carers. For example, the Newcastle United Learning Centre provides family learning in the context of football and this has raised levels of participation amongst men in particular (Haggart, 2001).

EVIDENCE FOR THE WIDER BENEFITS OF FAMILY LEARNING

Numerous family learning initiatives have been evaluated. Most evaluations are of local programmes and although they give rich insights into the wider benefits of these programmes, it is unclear whether the conclusions apply to other examples of family learning. Here we present just a few evaluations, focusing upon broader examples such as the National Foundation for Educational Research (NFER)'s evaluations of Family Literacy and Family Numeracy, the evaluation by the Community Education Development Centre (CEDC) of Share, and evaluations of some other particularly interesting projects. We begin with a summary of the wider benefits of family learning reported by Ofsted.

Ofsted's report of family learning (2000) focuses upon programmes based in schools, most of which offered family learning in literacy and numeracy, although some offered wider and more flexible curricula. Ofsted report that successful programmes of family learning offer good value for money and result in benefits for parents and children. Parents benefit from: improved competence in literacy and numeracy; progression for over 50 per cent of participants to FE and training or more challenging jobs; and increased confidence in contacts with schools, teachers, and the education system, which lead to more active partnerships with schools. They also acquire a greater understanding of child development and of the strategies that can be used to help children to learn at key points in development; improve their parenting; and develop better relationships with children. Children benefit from: accelerated development of oracy and pre-literacy skills; improved standards in numeracy and literacy; positive behavioural and attitudinal changes; and enhanced confidence and self-esteem. They also become more aware that learning is a normal activity throughout life and gain pleasure from collaborative learning.

Many of the family learning programmes inspected by Ofsted were funded partly at least by the Basic Skills Agency (BSA). Their Family Literacy Programme, directed at primary school children aged three to six whose parents have basic skills needs, involves inviting parents into the school to work with their children to help them with their reading. The NFER's evaluation of the pilot programme found benefits in terms of boosting children's literacy, parents' literacy and parents' ability and confidence to help their children (Brooks *et al.*, 1996). Communication between parents and children improved markedly and parents reported considerable improvements in their ability to communicate with their children's teachers. In terms of widening participation, the programmes appeared to be particularly successful in recruiting parents who had not studied since leaving school. An evaluation of the impacts of family learning upon families from linguistic minorities with children aged three to six reports similar outcomes (Brooks *et al.*, 1999).

A follow-up study revealed that improvements in children's literacy, in parents' literacy, and parents' abilities to help their children had lasted (Brooks *et al.*, 1997). Moreover, almost all parents felt that they had benefited in other ways, especially in terms of confidence and communication skills. High proportions of parents continued with further education, had entered work, and the rate of involvement of Family Literacy parents with their children's schools was double that of parents in a control group. Overall, Family Literacy parents 'continued to widen their participation in education and in society generally' (Brooks *et al.*, 1997: 10). An evaluation of Family Numeracy programmes reports similar findings (Brooks *et al.*, 1999).

Share is a family learning initiative developed by the CEDC which provides learning materials for children and their parents to work with from home. Parents can receive accreditation through the Open College Network. The model was implemented for Key Stage 1 in July 1996 in six local education authorities (LEAs). A measure of its perceived success is that it has expanded to cover Key Stages 1 and 2 in more than 40 LEAs, and implementation at Key Stage 3 is being piloted. Evaluations of the project demonstrate benefits in terms of parents' progression to further education and in children's attitudes to learning and their attainment (Bastiani, 1999; Lewis, 2000).

Bookstart provides free books and other resources that encourage parents to share books with their babies and preschool children. The initiative was evaluated from the outset and there have been a number of follow-up studies. Research findings derived from two main sources – a longitudinal study of children and parents involved in the initial Bookstart project based in Birmingham and smaller scale evaluations of 27 individual Bookstart projects – are consistent. They demonstrate positive benefits in terms of babies' competence with books, parents' attitudes towards books, rates of library membership, and performance at Key Stage 1 in both literacy and numeracy (Moore and Wade, 1998).

FAST (Families and Schools Together) is an early-intervention preventative school-based family support programme for children identified as having behavioural problems, which involves play therapy and family therapy. McDonald *et al*. (1997) evaluated the intervention and demonstrated that both children and parents benefit. Children of families who have participated in the programme have improved conduct, less anxiety and withdrawal and a better attention span, whilst participating parents meet friends through the project, enter employment, return for further education, and become more involved in their communities, including the school.

Research findings reported during the 1990s suggest that boys were performing less well than girls in all literacy-related tasks during that period. One reason for boys' underachievement may be that fathers tend to be less involved in their children's learning than mothers. Evaluations of some family learning projects (for example Lewis, 1999) report little involvement from fathers. In response, a national partnership administered by the Basic Skills Agency (BSA) has set up a Fathers and Reading project, which aims to encourage fathers to become more involved in their children's learning. The project's main focus is upon group work with fathers, which helps them to develop ways of supporting their children's learning. A learning pack is used which reflects male interests. The pilot project has been evaluated, and although few fathers participated (52 completed a pre-project questionnaire and 15 completed a post-project questionnaire), the findings are encouraging. As a result of the project, fathers' awareness of the importance of encouraging and supporting their children's learning grew, and they developed a better understanding of what it means to share reading with a child. In addition, library membership grew and fathers became more aware of their own learning needs (CEDC, 2001).

These and other evaluations demonstrate that family learning is beneficial across generations in a variety of ways. They also reveal the diversity of programmes that fall under the umbrella of family learning. What the Ofsted report on family learning concludes is that 'an evaluation of the long-term impact of family learning is long overdue' (Ofsted, 2000: 7). Such an evaluation should encompass the relative impacts of different types of family learning schemes (for example, in terms of formality, breadth and prescriptiveness of curricula), which types of family learning schemes suit which sorts of families, and the impacts of multiple agency funding and involvement. Much is already known in these areas, but there is a need to review this knowledge and build upon it in a systematic way to generate a fuller understanding of the strengths of family learning and to build a clearer vision for the future.

The research described here does not evaluate specific family learning projects. Instead, it seeks to unpack some of the pertinent issues and themes relating to family learning through gaining a purchase on the perspectives of families. The particular questions asked address what family learning might look like to families, their expectations of family learning, how they want it to happen and where, what they might get out of it, and what is the right way to describe it. It was decided that a series of focus group discussions with 'participating' and 'non-participating' parents would be the best way to achieve these aims.

Chapter 2

Research Methodology

RECRUITING RESEARCH PARTICIPANTS

The fieldwork for this research involved initially contacting the family learning co-ordinator for a London borough to request her assistance with recruiting local parents for this research. At the same time the literacy and numeracy consultants in the same borough were contacted to see if they too could be of any help (the email that was sent to the numeracy consultant can be seen in Appendix 1.1). The family learning co-ordinator indicated that she was unable to help and thus the search was focused on an alternative London borough. This prompted contact with the lifelong learning co-ordinator within the education department there (the email and attachment letter that was sent can be seen in Appendices 2.1 and 2.2), who was found to be very co-operative. In a meeting with one of her colleagues, the research was explained, with emphasis placed on the need to interview parents from a range of backgrounds and diversity of experience who had participated in a range of family learning courses, as well as parents who had not participated in a family learning course. The colleague then took on the responsibility of contacting the teachers who were running family learning courses at a number of centres within the borough, and distributing the flyer that had been designed to give parents more information about the research (an example of which can be seen in Appendix 3.1).

Focus group discussions were timetabled thereafter, during which the first author would talk to parents who had participated in family learning courses at a nursery school, a primary school, a secondary school and a family support centre. These were scheduled to take place at the location in which the family learning course was run, during the normal class time. Two focus group discussions were also set up to talk to parents who had not participated in a family learning course, at an early years centre and a primary school. All of these institutions were spread widely throughout the borough.

In the meantime, the numeracy consultant who had been contacted in the original London borough replied to say that she would welcome a researcher at her two groups to ask the parents there whether they would like to participate in a focus group discussion. During each of these visits both groups of parents agreed to be 'interviewed' during their next class the following week.

RESEARCH INSTRUMENTS

Two 'topic guides' were developed from which to steer each discussion: one for use with participating parents, and one for use with non-participating parents. These were designed to allow parents to talk about learning and family learning in general, before probing deeper into their attitudes towards and experiences of family learning. These can be found in Appendices 4.1 and 4.2. These guides were designed in order to allow each discussion to last for between one hour and one and a half hours, depending on the number of participants.

PROCEDURE

The fieldwork was undertaken during late February and early March 2001, when each group of parents was visited to carry out the focus group discussions. In each instance the family learning teacher was asked to leave the room, to allow parents' freedom of expression, and attempts were made to ensure that the room was not disturbed by other staff, parents or children. In one exception, where all participants spoke English as a second language, the teacher remained present to assist translation. After organising the parents into a group around a table, upon which the recording equipment was placed, the first author introduced herself, explained briefly what the purpose of the discussion was, and obtained consent to tape record the session. Following this, the tape recorder was switched on and participants were asked to introduce themselves in turn, as an 'ice-breaker'. A discussion was then developed from there with reference to the relevant topic guide.

Each group of parents that were encountered appeared to be quite anxious when first met. Some were still involved in their class activities and kept their heads down in an attempt to focus on their work and avoid eye contact. Once the first author had introduced herself and asked the parents to form a circle around the recording equipment, they seemed to relax far more and became less suspicious of her presence and motives. Thereafter she found it very easy to quickly build up a good rapport with each group, the members of which were comfortably able to express some very personal thoughts and feelings.

The parents in each group discussion largely agreed with each other. They seemed to raise very similar issues and were able to develop a train of thought amongst themselves. There was only one instance where disagreement occurred, between two women regarding how to encourage other parents to attend family learning courses. Thus the parents interviewed seemed to have formed very similar opinions of their experiences, which they discussed in a respectful fashion.

One of the meetings that had been arranged with a group of non-participants at an early years centre had to be cancelled owing to illness, and an attempt to rearrange this group discussion was unsuccessful. In addition, one of the group discussions arranged at a primary school was attended by only two parents, who arrived separately, and thus two in-depth interviews were carried out in its place. The results reported here are therefore based upon five focus group discussions with family learning course participants, two in-depth interviews with family learning course participants, and one focus group discussion with non-participating parents.

Chapter 3

Results From 'Participants'

CHARACTERISTICS OF PARENTS

The parents were aged between 24 and 50 years. There were 26 females and one male. Although the courses were populated mainly by females, there were one or two males that, apparently, attended each course. However, it was a matter of circumstance that on the days the focus group discussions were carried out, overall, only one male attended. Nineteen of the parents were married; four were cohabiting; four were single. They had a total of 63 children, each parent having between one and five children aged between five months and 19 years. The age of the parents at their first birth was between 16 and 35 years. One parent was in full-time work, two were in part-time work and 24 were not employed, two of whom were in part-time education.

Tables 3.1 and 3.2 below show the ethnicities and education of the parents.

Table 3.1 Ethnicities of the participating parents

Ethnicity	Number of parents
White British	14
Afro-Caribbean	3
Pakistani	2
Indian	1
Bangladeshi	1
Sri Lankan	1
Arab	1
Nepalese	1
Egyptian	1
Turkish	1
Polish	1

Table 3.2 Education of the participating parents

School leaving age	Number of parents
Dropped out at 15	2
Left at 15 and went on to YTS	1
Left at 16 with City and Guilds/CSEs	3
Left at 16 with O levels	2
Left at 18 with no qualifications	1
Left at 18 with O levels	1
Left at 18 with A levels	1
Left at 18 – qualifications unknown	1
Went to FE college and gained vocational qualifications	5
Possess sub-degree qualifications (diploma/HNC)	3
Possess first degree	2
Possess master's degree	3
Qualifications/school leaving age unknown	2

CHARACTERISTICS OF COURSES

Summary

There were six courses, four of which were numeracy and two literacy. At the time of the research, five were still in progress and one had finished. The courses lasted between three and four months, and parents attended one or two sessions a week, which took two to seven hours. There was an average of three to eleven regular attenders per course, from an original seven to fifteen.

Detail

Table 3.3 Details of family learning courses in London borough 1

	Course 1	**Course 2**
Location	Nursery centre	Primary school
Frequency	Once a week	Once a week
Length	3 months	3 months
Time	2 hours each session	2 hours each session
Time split	First hour with children, second hour with parents	First hour with children, second hour with parents
Staff	Teacher, nursery assistant	Teacher, nursery assistant
Original number of parents attending	12	Unknown
Current/final number of parents attending	6	6
Age of children participating	Preschool/nursery age	Preschool/nursery age
Content	Numeracy	Numeracy
Activities with children	Learn how children are taught; counting; drawing; colouring; shop prices; take a maths game home each week from the toy library	Learn how to teach children; colours, shapes and sizes; counting songs; days of the week; growing seeds; take a maths game home each week from the toy library
Activities for parents	Make counting games, make clocks, create a folder of work	Make counting games and board games; create a folder of work

	Course 1	Course 2
Certification	Certificate of attendance and achievement awarded	Unknown
Number of parents involved in research	3	5
Education of parents involved in research	1 with basic educational qualifications	1 with master's degree; 1 with BSc; 1 with vocational college qualifications; 2 with basic education

Table 3.4 Details of family learning courses in London borough 2

	Course 3	Course 4	Course 5	Course 6
Location	Primary school	Family support centre	Secondary school	Nursery school
Frequency	Once a week	Twice a week	Twice a week	Once a week
Length	4 months	4 months	3 months	3.5 months
Time	2.5 hours each session	3 hours each session	3.5 hours each session	2.5 hours each session
Time split	First 2 hours with parents, last half hour with children	First 2 hours with parents, last hour with children	First 2 hours with parents, last 1.5 hours with children	Half the group are with the children and half on their own; they swap halfway through the session
Staff	Teacher	Teacher, nursery assistant	Teacher, class assistant	Teacher, nursery assistant
Original number of parents attending	8	7	15	15
Current/final number of parents attending	3	5	12	11
Age of children participating	Preschool/ nursery age	Preschool/ nursery age	11–14 years	Preschool/ nursery age
Content	Numeracy (evaluation form completed at start to assess abilities)	Literacy	Literacy	Numeracy

contd

Table 3.4 Details of family learning courses in London borough 2 (contd)

	Course 3	Course 4	Course 5	Course 6
Activities with children	Play counting games; sing songs	Watch them; listen to them; interact/play with them; monitor their motor skills and co-ordination	Read, write and speak English; story writing; essay writing; family tree; autobiography; computer work; trip to Science Museum	Interact/play with children; learn how to teach them; trip to local library
Activities for parents	Learn maths, tax, insurance, budgeting; make counting games, cubes; create a folder of work	'Word power'; communication; directions; map reading; write an autobiography; fill in forms; write formal letters; write an evaluation at the end of each session of what children enjoyed and learnt; create a folder of work	Read, write and speak English; fill in forms, e.g. job applications; letter writing	General maths depending on ability level – volume, fractions, percentages, prices; create a folder of work
Certification	Certificate of achievement awarded	City and Guilds certificate awarded	Certificate of achievement awarded	Certificate of achievement awarded
Number of parents involved in research	2	5	4	8
Education of parents involved in research	Both left school at 18; 1 with A levels	1 with vocational college qualifications; 4 with basic educational qualifications	1 with teaching degree and economics degree; 1 with nursing qualification; 2 with basic educational qualifications	1 with master's degree; 1 with BA; 2 with sub-degree qualifications; 3 with college-level qualifications; 1 left school at 16 with O levels

CHARACTERISTICS OF THE AREAS IN WHICH COURSES WERE LOCATED

London borough 1

The first London borough has a very diverse population living in a fairly even mix of public and private housing. The proportion of owner-occupied households has risen rapidly during the last decade. About 24 per cent of the local population is from ethnic minorities and there has recently been a high influx of refugees and asylum seekers, who lack basic skills and English as a second language.

This borough is ranked as more deprived than London borough 2, yet it has a fairly even number of the most deprived and the least deprived wards in London. Many people commute into the borough for work; however, the unemployment compares unfavourably to the greater London average (5.6 per cent). However, here again the variations across the borough are huge, with some wards having a rate of less than 5 per cent and some wards having more than 11 per cent. Although there are many adults with level 4 qualifications in this borough, a large minority have no educational qualifications of any kind.

The borough also exhibits a contrast in its physical environment. It has numerous conservation areas covering a large percentage of the borough and contains many listed buildings. There is a wealth of townscapes from urban villages, through more inner city-style environments, to commercial and business areas.

London borough 2

The second London borough is very heavily populated and, not unlike London borough 1, there is a diverse ethnic mix with a quarter of inhabitants from minority ethnic origin, including asylum seekers. There is also a small yet growing proportion who are claiming homelessness. Many people also commute into this borough for work and to visit the large retail centre and cultural and tourist facilities.

Social and economic deprivation is unevenly distributed across the borough, with some electoral wards being amongst the most deprived in London. The unemployment rate is close to the average for all London boroughs, yet, as with deprivation, there are pockets of higher unemployment in some parts. A large number of resident lone parents are on income support, and the borough has a large number of housing benefit claimants.

PARENTS' COMMENTS

The major themes and issues arising from the main discussion topics are listed below. Where relevant, responses have been grouped or classified together under a heading, or positioned along a continuum, the ends of which have been labelled. In addition, salient quotes made by the parents have been included to demonstrate and contextualise the issues raised. Analysis showed that the views expressed were very similar regardless of course type or location, and owing to this, and the fact that a small number of parents were involved, no explicit reference will be made as to which issues were raised in which location and by whom. In the few instances where there was a demarcation in the types of comments made and the educational attainment of those making them, this is indicated.

What is learning?

Learning was seen by some as something which was very structured and organised, based in a formal educational setting, whereas others saw it in broader terms, encompassing a more informal and less structured concept.

Parents' responses to the question 'What is learning?'

Practical/formal/educational	More informal, less structured
A hassle	When you're older it's your choice
Disciplined	Doing something new
Being at school	Encouraging/helping others and your children
When structured or formal you have less choice	Fun, exciting, interesting
Achieving – a qualification	Expressing – being aware of your capabilities and knowing yourself
Gaining knowledge and skills enabling you to • take exams • get a job	Personal qualities • becoming a respectable human being • learning skills to progress in the outside world • acquiring social skills – interacting with others • gaining self-confidence
	Improving yourself – not just about gaining a qualification

Discipline. You have to discipline yourself to be able to learn. If you don't want to do it then you can't – you won't be able to do it.

(Lucy)

What is family learning?

Family learning was seen by some as something very home-based, relating to parents helping children with schoolwork or reading. Others had a much more global sense of family learning, perceiving it as something involving extended family members and friends, and taking place just about anywhere. Most believed it to be the transmission of knowledge from older generations to younger generations; only one (well-educated) parent believed that family learning involved the transmission of knowledge in the opposite direction.

Parents' responses to the question 'What is family learning?'

Playing with your children
Discussing things at the dinner table
Education starts in the family – children imitate parents and so parents are the role models
Encouraging your children – answering their questions
Helping your children with reading, writing, numbers, English, maths
Teaching your children what *not* to do
Setting aside time to be with your children – learning as a unit
Making learning enjoyable for your children
Understanding what your children do in school – being involved in their learning
Learning from your children
Activities with grandparents – for example, gardening, reading stories
Getting the whole family involved – helping the children
Life in general – everything you need to be a good person

You learn to set aside time to be with the children … family learning is learning as a unit. It could be anything from learning to interact with each other on different levels … when you're sitting down of an evening with your children doing maths and English and reading and things like that. Just being with them all the time, teaching them what you can.

(Tina)

Learning together. Just because we're adults, doesn't mean that we've learnt everything and as our children come through school, I'm sure that we'll be learning things through them.

(Harriet)

It teaches you a different opinion of yourself. I know mine do. Since teaching them I've definitely got a different opinion of me.

(Phoebe)

Who is involved in family learning?

It was apparent here that some parents do not have access to a wider support network which for others supplies additional family members to participate in family learning activities.

Parents' responses to the question 'Who is involved in family learning?'

Just me
- no contact or help from the father
- other family members not interested
- other family members a bad influence
- other family members live too far away

Me and my partner

Grandparents

Siblings – depends on ages?

Godparents

Friends

Doctors, health visitors

People in the street

People on television

Everybody

In my case I'm just by myself – we don't have any help from the father ... It's quite a hard job on me, like, I have to do everything by myself. So it's like, I do feel something missing with her father not being around.

(Afet)

Me! You've got doctors, health visitors, they're all involved in family learning. Even friends. [Grandparents] treat them differently, they've got experience, [they] play with them – they have a better understanding of them; they've already done it and got more knowledge and more time.

(Kayleigh)

It can be part of a crowd – other family members, like grandparents, their uncles, or even cousins – they can learn from their cousins, from their friends, from everyone.

(Jambayang)

Where does family learning take place?

As previously mentioned, family learning was perceived by a few parents as primarily a home-based experience. However, the majority recognised that family learning, like learning, could take place almost anywhere. As a result, the issues raised here have been placed on a spectrum from local to global.

**Parents' responses to the question
'Where does family learning take place?'**

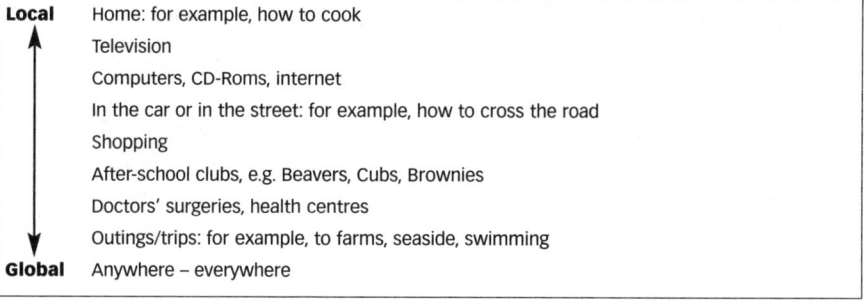

Local	Home: for example, how to cook
	Television
	Computers, CD-Roms, internet
	In the car or in the street: for example, how to cross the road
	Shopping
	After-school clubs, e.g. Beavers, Cubs, Brownies
	Doctors' surgeries, health centres
	Outings/trips: for example, to farms, seaside, swimming
Global	Anywhere – everywhere

We do a lot on the internet, I have to admit. Because my mum's not up on the internet she likes to go on to it with Philip and he's a lot better than me, unfortunately, but I'm learning through that as well.

(Sue)

It depends on whether you make it a learning experience. You know, walking down the road I often draw Lewis's attention to things like the fact that the leaves are starting to grow and we talk about spring, so it's just sort of starting to pay attention to what's happening around us.

(Harriet)

What involvement do you have in your child(ren)'s learning/education?

I helped in the nursery ... [My daughter] was in the playgroup before she came here and it was a hassle having to go every week, but it was something I enjoyed because I got to see her playing and learning and that was one of the drawbacks when she came here – you took her in the morning and you came and picked her up and you didn't know what happened in between. So now I don't do nothing to be honest to help the school in any way.

(Phoebe)

Parents' reponses to the question 'What involvement do you have in your children's learning/education?

Home	Outside	School
Playing with toys, reading stories, listening to children read, writing, counting, singing songs	Going to playgroups	No involvement in the school/nursery at all
	Going to the park	Going to parents' evenings
Helping them with their homework	Swimming, ice skating, bike riding	Going to the school to discuss progress/problems with teachers
Asking them what is going on at school – talking about their day	Sponsoring school activities	Going into school as a classroom helper
		Being a school and national governor

What motivates you to learn?

Many parents identified reasons for wanting to learn which were related to themselves rather than their children. These were either practical, with tangible outcomes, or personal, with more emotional or spiritual consequences. Some parents reported that they were more motivated to learn because of their children.

Parents' responses to the question 'What motivates you to learn?'

Self		Children
Practical	**Personal**	
Achieve • a qualification/certificate • better job or go back to work • better quality/standard of living from improved employment and increased earnings	Do something for yourself • improve yourself – be a better person • self-satisfaction or pride from improvement • have own goals and aims Cope better with life – be more confident Social interaction with others Stimulation – something to do	Enjoyment from watching children learn To gain respect from children – set them a better example Teach children more and prepare them better for life Give children a better future Awareness that it is my responsibility to educate the children – no one else is available to fulfil this role Avoid a repeat of history – do better than my own parents did To understand the education system better

When I think about learning now it's for the children ... it's like trying to get all the information they need to just do what they need to do. When they finish school they go out into the big wide world, so they can achieve all of the knowledge that they need ... Just to set a good example to the children, to show them that, and to provide for them as well, to go to work ... It's about you doing something and achieving something; you're achieving something for yourself – your own goal. To have social interaction with others. Getting a better education for my children than I had.

(Ellen)

I don't like feeling like a dead-head … just to get somewhere near that goal [of being an accountant] because I'm miserable if I don't meet my goals … Eventually in a year or two I want to go back to work … I don't want a kitchen job or things like that anymore, I've decided already just through doing this course and realising that I can count, and them things, that I don't want that sort of job … I want to start working my way back up to being confident enough to go for interviews for office jobs … To give my kids a better future and financial support … I want to be a better role model.

(Tina)

My mum couldn't help me when I left school, couldn't help me with my homework. She didn't have a good education and I don't want it to be the same for my daughter.

(Andrea)

I'm interested in children's education. I want them to be good educated persons and good, better citizens, so I joined these sessions so I can get involved with my children. And want to learn the system you know because this is … I'm not educated here or studied here. I want to help my children. I want to improve myself as well. It will improve myself and my children will get benefit from this … I want to help my children … and if they will be good persons, good education, it will be reward for me and it will be better for the future. I will feel proud if they will do good, and I'm struggling for this.

(Mena)

It's nice to see their surprise and their interest and just their wonder … we took Philip to the zoo recently and he was just so fascinated by it – why they were where they were and how they grew and that sort of thing – he just really enjoyed it … One of the ladies here was pregnant and she let him touch her tummy and his eyes were really big because he could feel the baby moving around – he's just fascinated. I enjoy seeing that.

(Sue)

Education is very empowering, you feel that [because] you're being offered the opportunity that it almost means you can do it because they're saying, 'Here it is, have a go!'

(Taniesha)

I think knowledge gives you confidence too. It makes you feel [like] the person who *does* know ... I went back [to college] a couple of years ago and while I was on the course I felt like a completely different person. I wasn't just their mum – I was somebody else as well. It does alter your personality.

(Lucy)

What are the barriers to learning?

Most parents quoted practical and course-related reasons as the barriers to their learning. Some parents referred to psychological reasons – things within themselves – and these views tended to be conveyed by the less well-educated parents. Only one (highly educated) parent explicitly stated that there were no barriers to her learning, which she explained was mainly because her children could now take care of themselves so that she had the time to pursue qualifications and courses.

Boredom. If it's boring or I can't understand it, I won't even bother ... Some people treat me stupid; you say you're doing extra English at our ages, 'What do you want to do that for? What you don't know now you're never going to know!', and I think if you're put down enough you won't do it.

(Jeannette)

You've got to find a place where you can go and where the children are looked after whilst you're doing the course, or where the children are at school and you can come and do the course and not be put under pressure – you've got time to do the work ... It's no good having a big group. The teacher needs to be able to get round to everybody.

(Davina)

Parents' responses to the question 'What are the barriers to learning?'

Practical	Self-related	Other-related	Course-related
Lack of time – juggling commitments of parenthood, housework, work, studying and so on Lack of support for childcare – physical and financial No peaceful environment in which to study	Bad experiences from previous learning Embarrassment due to lack of skills and abilities Low confidence and low self-esteem Lack of will power	Children – guilt at leaving them Other people's negative attitudes Lack of support – emotional	Costs • enrolment, tuition fees, equipment • travelling to the course Institutional policies on childcare Lack of information on courses available Poor accessibility – too far away Poor availability Time it takes to complete a course or get a qualification Content • too hard • too boring Taught in large groups Personality clash with those running courses

[Lack of] encouragement. If you're disencouraging me in something – if you say, 'You're not learning, you cannot understand' – if you show me that behaviour, I do not go, I don't want to.

(Rashida)

You can't afford to go to college or university because you can't pay the fees, you can't pay the childcare because you're not working because you're studying so it's just like a no-win situation. It wouldn't have to be so much 'free' – you don't mind paying something but you ... I personally went when my daughter was young, I did go to college again then. They had a crèche there and I paid £2.50 a week, so once she was out of nappies she could go in there and that was fine. She started when I started and she finished when I finished and I could afford £2.50, £3.00 a week, that was fine – give them their lunch – but now it's not like that. They have to be over a certain age for the colleges to take on responsibility – it really isn't as easy as it seems.

(Phoebe)

What are the benefits to you from attending the course?

These were very quickly identified and discussed at length. Most parents could see that the benefits gained were multiple, relating either to themselves in some way or to others.

Parents' responses to the question 'What are the benefits to you from attending the course?'

Child-related	Other-related	Self-related	
		Practical	**Emotional**
How to teach my child (for example, language to use) Raised awareness of opportunities where I can teach my child Better understanding of my child's weaknesses Involvement in something my child does Quality one-to-one time with my child in a different environment • see more of their personality • strengthens the bond between us Understand how children are being taught today Appreciation of how much input is needed in child's learning	Get a break from the children Talking point at end of the day with partner Meeting others • working together as a team • feeling special because we're a separate unit • exchanging views and learning about others' experiences • making friends • developing a support network – helping with each others' problems	Learning things for myself • new knowledge • revision of things already learnt • can teach others Gaining a certificate or qualification – pride at accomplishment Creating a foundation to build upon – progression to other courses or employment Increased motivation to learn and progress	Gaining more confidence – regaining independence and individuality Feeling more 'alive' Challenging my mind – awakening my brain No longer feeling stupid Release from normal daily life • separate time just for me • prevents boredom and depression • more relaxed and less likely to shout at children

I already know my brain is starting to wake up and I feel a better person for it. By doing something like this it's made me feel more like my old self, the person I like being. It's already making me feel ready to be capable enough of branching off into doing other courses ... It's made me feel more alive in my own way, got my brain going, given me more self-confidence, motivation big time. It's also a release from my day-to-day normal living, you know, it's like a little social gathering as well ... it's important to me, it has done a lot for me ... I'm starting to get a direction in life.

(Tina)

You get a better understanding of what [the children] do [at school]. You can help them in that aspect ... You also meet people, lots of different people. You get a better understanding of what everyone else is going through. The learning is a bonus ... you've got a nice support network. I mean, if you've got a problem, you can approach the people that are teaching you or you've got another parent doing the course with you that will help ... When you get a piece of paper to say you've passed, it's a lovely feeling.

(Kayleigh)

We break ... for about half an hour, with a coffee and that's when we sort of chat; if we've got problems we chat. So, not only are we doing English but we're also helping ourselves emotionally ... we know it doesn't go any further than the room and we can all talk openly.

(Jeannette)

For the first time I went to the 24-month check-up with my daughter by myself without taking anyone [to interpret] – I was very proud.

(Yasmeen)

I came to know other parents as well and I came to know that they have also difficulties and it relieves my pressure – it's not just me! I'm not the one only, you know, there are other people as well who have problems.

(Mena)

I quite like being ... playing a small part of Kathryn's nursery because she says to me, 'Oh is it a numeracy day today?' – she likes the fact that I'm here ... You're seeing them in this environment, where, I think, they change. They're really independent; it's really exciting for parents to see your child thriving like that without you and just to see how they learn and ask other people questions. Plus, I actually like coming in and doing activities here because you feel a part of the whole learning process that they're experiencing.

(Chullaki)

Quality time because we do things here that we then go home and have to involve our children in, say if we've made a game and we play it with them. There is this sort of hidden agenda but it's a game to them, so they learn, so maybe you wouldn't have done that game with them [before the course] ... I see the advantages now, which has taken quite a long time to come to fruition, but now I see them ... you get more confident ... and these are the hidden benefits of the course.

(Taniesha)

My daughter's personality. I've seen more of her personality since I've been seeing her at school. She's very different at home to how she is at school – it's like two completely different children. My dad brought her to school the other day and said once they got through the school gates, it wasn't like it was Georgia. She's a completely different child, very, very different. Like indoors she kind of floats around – she's like a little airhead, you know, nothing kind of goes in – but when she's at school she's kind of focused on things ... At home I was getting frustrated with her because I was trying to sit with her, trying to do things – 'I just don't want to, I just can't', you know – but when I come into the school and I do it with her I feel like I can do it better.

(Phoebe)

What are the benefits to your child(ren) from you attending the course?

Again, all parents could quickly identify multiple benefits accruing to their children from participating in an organised family learning initiative. The less well-educated parents recognised the social benefits more than the emotional benefits to their children.

Parents' responses to the question 'What are the benefits to your child(ren) from you attending the course?

Practical	Social	Emotional	Parental
Improved • knowledge (for example maths, writing) transferred to other environments • speech (vocabulary and pronunciation) • behaviour (calmer) • concentration/attention 'Jumping the queue' – access to speech therapist sooner than normal New games to play with, made on the course Better prepared for school	Improved socialising – mixing with adults and children – sharing Improved relationship with teachers at school Making friends with other children More tolerant of children from different backgrounds – can see own parent interacting with their parents	Confidence Security from parent's presence	Parents available to translate unfamiliar words One-to-one attention received from parents – children feel special Learning that education does not stop after school – see parents as better role models

The one-to-one interaction is great because I don't get a lot of time to give him the time and attention that he needs – it's just one-to-one for a solid hour, trying to absorb it all ... I can see my son's definitely learning from it, I mean, once a day he'll pick up on something he learnt in the group ... So it pushes me to carry on with it because I can see he's really benefiting from it, really gaining.

(Ellen)

You can communicate more with them and you can understand at their level what they're doing.

(Sandra)

Socialising, because my daughter, she don't go to many people, she's very clingy and coming here, it's helped her ... My daughter has got a speech problem ... special language disorder, and trying to mix her with other children might encourage her to talk.

(Davina)

My children, very very happy and improved ... English, spelling, writing – better. Computers ... Better in stories and better in English, writing and interested in education. His education is better and better with his teacher ... [The day] before [the course] the children are very interested, before they want to know, tomorrow, 'Don't forget!'

(Rafiq)

My daughter loves it – 'Are you coming with me today?' and it does make them feel really special – they're really waiting for the class.

(Henka)

The friendships that are formed, which I think benefit your child – to be in an environment where they feel they have more than one good friend. It's such a good thing, they feel that their confidence is strengthened, you get more confident but they do too, and these are the hidden benefits of the course.

(Taniesha)

Yes – they like the sound ... that they're special. It's nice for them to know that we're thinking about them ... for them to come in and they see you wandering around the school, they know you're taking part in their life even though they're not there in the kitchen with you. It does make a big difference to them. A big difference.

(Phoebe)

What are the benefits to others from you attending the course?

Most of the parents could see that there were possible benefits to other people. These were mainly discussed in terms of those who might benefit from the passing on of information learnt during the course, as well as future educators of their developmentally accelerated children.

It makes us more relaxed – we're not so tense with children ... You're able to answer questions when people ask. You think more now, whereas before your immediate reaction was, 'Haven't got a clue! Can't do it! Go away!'

(Jeannette)

Parents's responses to the question 'What are the benefits to others from you attending the course?'

Course-related	Others		Longer term
	In the home	**Outside the home**	
Course organisers – good attendance means more courses will be run The crèche – younger children spend time there while you and your older child take part in the course	Child's siblings – children teach them things they learnt on the course Partner – parents pass on information about how to teach children Grandparents – have better idea of how education system works today Cousins and friends – children show them how to play games made on the course	Everyone around me – family, friends, doctors, et cetera • I'm more independent and assertive • I communicate better • I'm less stressed/ tense • I can teach others what I have learnt	Future educators will benefit through less input required because • children already have basic skills • children more motivated to learn Whole system – society

Learning new methods that they teach now, these universal methods at school and the infant language, I'm passing that information on to my husband so that he's in a position to help our children as well. Even though he isn't attending the course, he benefits in a way, from passing on information.

(Chullaki)

The bodies that run these courses benefit because we participate so therefore they think that it's well worthwhile ... 'We'll do some more' and that they've found that here is an area that's sort of untapped, you know, where people are wanting to learn and I suppose, you know, in a way it just gives you a taste that when you pass that period where your children are so dependent upon you, it might just encourage you to go out there and learn a bit more. So in a bigger sense it benefits society at the end of the day because you've already had like a pre-liminary taste of a course.

(Taniesha)

What was it about the course that made it successful?

Virtually all of the parents spoke about the success of the course in terms of the qualities of the teachers tutoring them. The majority also cited the practicalities of the course as the cause of success.

Parents' responses to the question 'What was it about the course that made it successful?'

Practical	Other people
The crèche	Other students
• younger children are cared for, making the course accessible to more parents	• some were friends
• familiarity with people running it	• non-judgmental
	• had things in common
It was free!	• keen to learn and committed
	• worked as a team
The structure and organisation	
• the way it was advertised	The teacher
• the introductory letter explained what to expect	• supportive
• it was well planned and well laid out	• calm
	• encouraging
Diversity of activities – always interesting with games, songs, making things, borrowing things, trips outside	• good approach to children
	• also a parent
	• recognised capabilities
	• never superior
Choice given of what to study	• easy to get on with
	• not angry if a class missed
Flexibility – it was tailored to each person's ability	• helped with problems – a 'counsellor'
	• treated me as an individual and an adult
Small groups – lots of attention from the teacher	• not intimidating
Support available from an interpreter	
Friendly atmosphere – safe, informal and relaxed	
Accessibility – located in the community close to home	
Extended when it was clear that parents were keen to learn more	

[The teacher] is doing a good job, she's very supportive, she encourages [the children] nicely. She's a very calm person … she knows the way to talk to them and encourage them at the same time. Their attention is going away and she knows how to bring them back.

(Afet)

It's who we're with. There's no one that thinks they're too big-headed to be here ... Some of us knew each other anyway, we've seen each other about.

(Jeannette)

This is ideal when someone's looking after the kids ... your time's your own ... It helps when you've got keen pupils.

(Cindy)

She will group us, take our details of what we want and direct us. Some are on the basic level, some are on second level – I am on the third level ... She didn't tell anybody at the start we are starting all together and after that, little by little, she knows our levels.

(Vidu)

Also that it's with people that you know, even though you didn't know them very well before, you don't feel so limited about saying things or asking questions. You know, when you're in a room with strangers you just keep to yourself.

(Chullaki)

We're all at different levels. We've all got subjects that we want to brush up upon, fractions, so she's covering quite a lot but she'll make sure you understand without making you look thick.

(Beverley)

And it's a funny time when you have children, when you've been working and then you give up working and you have the children, you do lose a lot of confidence; you've been taken out of that environment where you feel confident and you know what you're doing. So even if you've been in a professional career before having your children, suddenly you do lose a lot of confidence and to actually go somewhere else with people you don't know – sounds silly – but it is quite a difficult thing. So this is a safe environment.

(Harriet)

What are the disadvantages to you from attending the course?

Only eight out of the 27 parents stated that there were any disadvantages and their comments related largely to the practicalities of the course.

Parents' responses to the question 'What are the disadvantages to you from attending the course?'

Practical	Emotional
Early mornings	When it ends I'll be bored/depressed
Managing my time and having to get myself organised	When I can't make it I feel guilty that I've let the others down
We won't have time to complete all units	
Trying to catch up on missed lessons	

We've still got another two stages to do – we've only got stage one behind us. We don't think they're going to fund it. [The centre manager] is quite prepared to let us do it, [the teacher] as far as we know, she hasn't got any other commitments, is quite prepared to take us through but we haven't got the funding ... I'd like to finish all the units ... [When I've missed a class] I feel like I'm letting people down ... as if I was letting these [other groups members] down.

(Jeannette)

When I've had to work then there's no ... way of catching up what you've missed out.

(Taniesha)

I find this morning a bit stressful ... we were aiming to get here at nine a.m., to do the activity with our children, and I found that difficult – you know with the two getting them ready and the traffic's really bad driving here because I have to bring the car on this day and then we go out straight from here, so I find it quite a busy morning, you know, to get everything ready.

(Harriet)

What are the disadvantages to your child(ren) from you attending the course?

More parents could identify disadvantages to their children than they could to themselves, but these were still small in number and related to the practical side of the course, i.e. things that could be changed.

Parents' responses to the question 'What are the disadvantages to your child(ren) from you attending the course?'

Immediate		Long-term
Practical	**Emotional**	
Missing school classes to attend the course	Feeling upset and deserted when parent has to a miss a class	When the course ends she'll leave her friends and miss them – perhaps regress to introversion again?
Repeating things in class time already learnt during the course		
Disruption to their routine – removal and return to nursery class		
My presence in the room makes her misbehave		
Being left with strangers – causes havoc		

> Only when you want to bring her back into the nursery and settling her down – she doesn't want to go back – that's the only thing for me. It takes a while to settle her back in.
>
> (Alison)

> She was so upset and I felt so awful that that's when it did become like a real responsibility ... I have to be there on a Tuesday morning because just seeing her, she was just so upset and once she's upset it really upsets me and I really felt I'd let her down.
>
> (Taniesha)

> I've noticed that what we've been doing here, about two weeks later they start to do the same thing downstairs in my daughter's class, so she's done it and she doesn't want to do it again and she starts to get distracted.
>
> (Phoebe)

What are the disadvantages to others from you attending the course?

Only four parents could think of disadvantages that might be experienced by other people owing to their participation in the course.

Parents' responses to the question 'What are the disadvantages to others from you attending the course?'

Other children
- younger ones left in crèche see less of parents than they used to
- school-aged children who missed the opportunity of family learning classes at nursery

Parents who can't attend the course due to
- lack of places
- lack of time, for example work commitments

> I feel bad for my other daughter because she's in Year One and she sees I spend this hour with Gemma and I'm not spending it with her.
>
> (Lucy)

How could the course be improved?

The improvements to the courses which parents recommended were largely practical. In most cases parents just wanted extra time in order to complete all of the units of work.

> None of us would sort of mind really if we were here Monday to Friday – it's that relaxing; that good … I think if you improved it too much it'd be too much pressure.
>
> (Jeannette)

> What you were saying about what sort of people they were targeting, I'm not sure that actually they've got the right people that they wanted. We're all really interested in our children's education anyway and we're all literate and numerate and all that but you know you were saying, that they were trying to target people that weren't. I think if you signed up for this sort of thing then you're that way inclined.
>
> (Chullaki)

Parents' responses to the question 'How could the course be improved?'

Practical	Other people
Timing – make it start later in the morning	Target parents who have literacy and numeracy problems
Make it longer • to run the length of a term • so that all units can be completed • so that more topics can be covered	
Make it more frequent	
Provide follow-up support and feedback	
Provide advance notice of what to expect the following week, to allow preparation	
Design it to cause the least disruption to the child's routine	

It would be better if it ran for the term rather than just for twelve weeks – if it started for the term because it's taken until up to now for the children to get into the routine, to know they're coming, to do their thing, for them all to be sitting down.

(Lucy)

What prevents your attendance?

The vast majority of parents stated that they really enjoyed the course and did not like to miss any classes. They tended to say that they did not attend only if there was a very good (practical) reason.

Parents' responses to the question 'What prevents your attendance?'

Visits from family members from abroad
Appointments • repair personnel • doctors/hospital
Family illness – caring for others
Going on holiday
Part-time work

What other courses have you attended?

About one third of the parents had been involved in other courses prior to their participation in the numeracy or literacy course they were discussing (none of whom possessed higher educational qualifications). Most of them had enjoyed the experience, and those that did not rated their current experience far more favourably.

Parents' responses to the question 'What other courses have you attended?'

Parenting Skills – without my children
• it was very good with lots of different speakers

Introduction to Preschool Practice
• I passed

Childcare

Health and Social Care

Literacy
• there was a crèche

English – evening classes
• not of any benefit because the large class was of different abilities and the teacher pitched it all at one level which I had already surpassed

Introduction to PCs
• I am enjoying it

Numeracy
• not so good because I didn't get the support from the teacher, so I dropped out
• dropped out because it was too much on top of the other two courses I'm doing but I will go back to it

Sign Language
• great fun but in a big group in a school atmosphere so less attention from the teacher
• very enjoyable with implications for future enhanced earnings

What other courses would you like to attend?

Virtually all parents said that they would take part in other courses. Often those on literacy courses identified numeracy as the next course they'd like to do and vice versa. Many cited computer courses as the next course they'd like to participate in because they felt the world of employment was dominated by computers and they recognised that their children were being taught computing from very early ages.

Parents' responses to the question
'What other courses would you like to attend?'

Any
- if childcare facilities were provided
- if there was one-to-one time with my child and they made progress
- if the course was free and accessible

Social skills, anger management

Parenting skills

Childcare

Child development

Literacy

French

Science

Health and safety

Computers – CLAIT

Home-related – sewing, dressmaking

Yoga, aqua aerobics

Numeracy

Every aspect of what is taught in schools

I've done one that was more based not on numbers but on letters. I'd attend anything where you were getting the one-to-one and they were actually gaining from it, learning and progressing, I'd try to attend, if he was gaining from it, improving and learning ...When [my younger one] reaches three I'll probably do more courses, find out what he's interested in.

(Ellen)

Hopefully I'm going to do a childcare course when this finishes; it's given me the confidence to do a childcare course ... I was doing City and Guilds maths at [a local] school and found it quite hard ... I wasn't getting as much help as what [our teacher] is giving us on this course.

(Cindy)

I've already got one certificate – Introduction to Preschool Practice –
I completed that one and passed it ... All day on a Friday I do
computers – 'Introduction to PCs'. When I finish that in April I'm
going to do a CLAIT one in September ... you have to do an exam ...
I'd try any course ... I was actually doing the maths number power
over at [a local training centre] but because I was doing this as well
I was finding it too difficult so I stopped that and I'm going to go
back to it ... she said you don't have to rush, take your time; I can go
back.

(Andrea)

How would you encourage others to attend?

A number of parents felt that there was a group of people that just could not
be persuaded to attend such courses because of their mental 'make-up'.
They felt that some people just will not attend if they:
• are in full-time work or education
• lack the motivation, will power or confidence
• had very bad experiences at school.
However, many reported a number of useful ways in which other
parents might be encouraged to attend and it was widely felt that the best
way was through word of mouth, i.e. hearing directly from parents who had
already been on a course. Interestingly, no parents cited the topic of the
family course as a variable that could be tweaked to encourage more people
to attend. For example, it might be supposed that more practical or physical
subjects might appeal more to a male audience, e.g. DIY, carpentry, car main-
tenance, football.

Parents' responses to the question
'How would you encourage others to attend?'

Practical		People-orientated
Course itself	**Information about the course**	
Run the courses at different times	Advertise it differently • emphasise the benefits to children rather than to parents • avoid wordy letters home • design colourful posters for notice boards • place an advert on a blackboard outside the school	Encourage attendance with a friend
Provide free crèche facilities		Open days
Make the courses free or supply information about funding		Word of mouth • tell others about your own experiences • show others your work folder
Keep the groups small and informal	Make clear and simple information available about what to expect	Emphasise • benefits to children • benefits to other family members – bonds strengthened • other benefits to self – different identity, meeting people, progression • not like school – no bullying, no superior teachers, will not look stupid • opportunity to catch up on what was missed at school

Other people, they haven't got as much will power or just haven't hit the right time in their life where they can stand up for themselves ... Another aspect of the course was I said to Kayleigh, 'Do you fancy it?' – Me and Kayleigh get on, we're friends ... and an extra bit of a boost or a bonus was the fact that I knew she was going to be sitting in here when I arrived so I wasn't just going to be walking in going, 'Oh God', you know, a room full of strangers ... You know what men are like – weird species! Egos, a lot of them ... Those that don't mind sitting on their arse and getting paid for doing nothing, they're going to go on doing it. They've got to have something there to make them want to branch out.

(Tina)

I think really the only way is an open day: let people come and see the work; let them talk to the teachers who'll be running the class; let them talk to the pupils that have done the exam or that particular course.

(Jeannette)

I'd say to people that it's very enjoyable here – learning is fun; that we do lots of writing as well as reading as well as speaking so all things are covered. It'll be good for you to learn English – come just once or twice to see what it's like so that you're not worried about it.

(Rafiq)

I think it comes down to people individually: if they want to be involved, if they're interested enough, they will do it; if not, they're not going to do it ... There's excuses for work, whereas I think there are ways around that.

(Jennie)

I do tend to sort of disagree with that thing about people that are like a certain group who'll never be interested because I went on the parenting courses and they were always really full because when you've been on them I think your exuberance of being on them to someone else encourages them to go because you're telling them at a different level ... you're telling them about your experience and once you tell someone about your experience of being involved, that sells it much more than reading it in black and white ... All those letters, you know, you get mounds and mounds of literature coming from this place ... Maybe a more visual thing, something more permanent in the nursery where you couldn't miss it, as opposed to a very unattractive black and white letter.

(Taniesha)

I think as far as dads go, because they are seen as the breadwinners most of them have to go out and work and everything like that. It's the way they've been brought up. If their dad's been the breadwinner then they see that and they've seen their mum doing the things with the kids then that's the way they've learnt, that's what they're going to do. You can try changing them a little bit – get them involved – but to actually get them to sit in a group ... and also, I could not imagine [my partner] sitting here with other women. He'd feel really out of place so I think it's because it's seen as the mums' group. [Single dads] would have to swallow a lot of their own pride I think to come in and, OK – that's a case of having to, not really wanting to.

(Lucy)

Other comments

The overall impression was that the parents had all enjoyed the courses they had been attending and thought that organised family learning initiatives were a very valuable resource that should be made more widely available.

Other comments made by parents

Family learning is fun

More people should be encouraged to participate

There should be easier access to information about courses

Education/learning does not have to be scary

Family learning is a good way to learn how the education system operates

Family learning is a good way to start on the road back to employment

Teachers really can make a difference

There should be more family learning courses – the government needs to allocate more funding

The workplace and education system is forever changing and family learning helps you get your foot back on the ladder

Family learning is a good way to start ... It helps you mould your children, I believe, for the better ... Eventually my kids are going to grow up and leave me; I don't want to be left sitting on my arse without a job doing nothing – not me.

(Tina)

It's good to be able to interact with your child in school, definitely. I didn't have it and I know – I think – if I did, if my mum and dad were more 'into' my education then I would have done a lot better ... I would have done more – been involved more, probably the after-school clubs or reading clubs or things that were going on rather than just not being able to wait to get out of the doors the minute the bell rang ... It's nice to break the ice as well with mothers and children from other countries. I'm not in the habit of just walking up to other people and going 'hello' and introducing myself but when you're put in this situation and your children see that you make friends, it's easier for them to make friends as well in the class. If they're in the class and they don't know anyone, they think, 'That's alright because my mum knows their mum so I'm going to play with them,' and it makes it easier for them to make friends.

(Phoebe)

TEACHERS' COMMENTS

These comments were made by a teacher who sat in on a focus group carried out with a group of parents who were all learning English as a second language. Their family learning course had been designed to improve their spoken, written and read English. The teacher was available during the discussion to translate any questions or answers, and was able to elaborate on some of the parents' comments as follows.

What about the course makes it successful?

There was a wide range of abilities. Yasmeen, who was beginners, never really attempted to speak English before she actually started attending the classes and she told me, 'Oh well I can't come I don't know any-thing,' and I said, 'Well that's exactly what we want – we want people who don't know anything.' Yasmeen attended regularly – she had wonderful attendance.

Disadvantages to children

When they did the joint lessons together we had to take the children out of another subject to have it during the day; that's what we had to do ... I had to be very careful who I picked to be on the course ... it's unavoidable.

How could the course be improved?

[Our school] puts on computers skills for parents in the evening but what we did during the day when they were working with their children, parents had access to computers as well. But one of the failings of our course was we didn't actually give them, the parents, a lot of time on the computers – the children had the time on the computers. This is something we are looking into, to actually give them, the parents, time to actually access the computers.

Why did others drop out of the course?

One person left the course who had an operation; one got a job two weeks into the class.

How to encourage others to attend

We've already heard from parents who've heard about the class and would like us to start another one. So we're thinking of starting another one for people who are not necessarily parents at our school but who are wanting to learn English ...We started with one more [dad] and we were hoping that Rafiq and him would gel together and keep coming together but he was unable to.

Comments from other teachers

The following comments were made by teachers, at the same school, on feedback forms completed after the course had been run. They were asked to indicate whether there had been any changes in the pupils who had attended the family learning literacy course in their normal curriculum classes. These forms were made available by the teacher who had interpreted during the focus group discussion with parents. It was not the purpose of this research to gather the comments of tutors running these courses; however, since the information became available fortuitously, it has been reported here.

Caleb and Khadiga both show greater confidence and are more motivated. They ask questions more readily and seem happier in lessons.

Caleb has definitely improved. He is doing a lot more written work. He likes the lesson and he has begun to answer questions. His confidence has grown.

Bharat and Suneet, two pupils who did not communicate much, are now more ready to ask and answer questions during the family literacy sessions as well as whole class situations. Their confidence in spoken and written English has improved. Khadiga and Caleb have both shown signs of increasing motivation in the work they do in the family literacy sessions and in their classwork, in English especially.

A direct comment made by another teacher was as follows:

Whilst I was at this school I met another one of the teachers who taught a pupil that took part in the family learning literacy course. She said that this child had new-found motivation and enthusiasm to learn. His confidence had grown and he was far more likely to raise his hand in class, even if he got the answer wrong. This she found particularly encouraging because he suffers from a speech impediment.

School newsletter publicity

The teacher who sat in on the focus group discussion provided a copy of the most recent school newsletter in which the progress made by the parents and pupils on the literacy course was reported. An excerpt from the newsletter, which demonstrates the manner in which this school helped to publicise the course, follows:

Family Literacy Project

Ten bilingual pupils and their parents have been enjoying improving their skills in English. This project funded by the Continuing Education and Training Service and [this] school has been a huge success. The pupils who have been part of the project felt they learnt something from their parents and enjoyed working with them. Parents felt involved in the education of their children and were able to support them in their learning. Congratulations to [the pupils] who have produced excellent folders of work about themselves and their country. These will be on display in the foyer. If you would like further information about the project please contact [the EAL co-ordinator]. We hope to run another next year.

CHILDREN'S COMMENTS

These comments were made by the pupils of the parents on the course described above, i.e. all were attending a school where the family learning course had been designed to help them and their parents improve their spoken, written and read English. They were thus all learning English as a second language. Their comments had been collected on feedback forms once the course had finished, which were again made available by the teacher who had interpreted during the focus group discussion with their parents. It was not the purpose of this research to gather the comments of children on these courses; once again, however, since the information became available fortuitously, it has been reported here.

> I haven't worked with my mother in this way. It has improved my relationship with my mother. I see her in another light … Old memories coming to my mind. I liked working with the other [similar ethnic group] children … Felt safe – more freedom.
>
> (Kaveri)

> It helped working in small bilingual group because everyone was doing work – no noise, more attention. I understood talk because others explained in my language.
>
> (Nilay)

> It had helped me and my mum because I got to learn lot of things about my mum and I also got to know some of my family story.
>
> (Yashini)

> I enjoyed … working with my mum … I got information from my mother and I never worked with my mother – new experience – liked it.
>
> (Ravi)

> I enjoyed having lesson with my mum because she can tell me what happen to me in the past. I like doing things in computer and learning English. I also like learning about my country and I learned here so I am enjoying … More information from my mother is family stories and what I am look like and what I do in the past and how I am born.
>
> (Bharat)

I think my work has been improved by 65 per cent in typing on the computer. Before I use to type by one hand but now I can type by two hands ... If it is a small group then people won't be shy to speak out and that is what I do.

(Nittila)

Chapter 4

Results From 'Non-Participants'

CHARACTERISTICS OF PARENTS

The parents were aged between 23 and 34 years. All four were female, White British and not employed. One was married, two were cohabiting and one was single. They had a total of 14 children, each parent having between two and five children aged between eight months and 15 years. Their age at the birth of their first child ranged from 18 to 23 years. Three had dropped out of school without any qualifications; one had left at 16 with CSEs.

Three out of four of these women had, whilst growing up, been a part of the care system and their present family units had experienced (or still were experiencing) heavy involvement from social services. Each one of these recalled having very bad experiences at school, as a result of which they had dropped out of school and were now lacking basic literacy and numeracy skills. All four women lived on a large local council estate.

PARENTS' COMMENTS

As in the previous section, the major themes and issues arising from the main discussion topics are listed below, with further categorisation/classification where relevant, along with any salient quotes made by the parents.

What is learning?

Similarly to the participating parents, these parents conceptualised learning as something formal and organised, as well as something more informal and less structured.

Parents' responses to the question 'What is learning?'

Going to school – getting a good education
Work – getting a good job
Getting on with life
Everything
Fun

Job – going to school, getting some A levels and getting a good job.

(Gloria)

It's work ... everything ... everything for your future.

(Rebecca)

What is family learning?

These parents also identified helping children at home with schoolwork as family learning, as well as recognising that many other activities can be described by the same term.

Things to do with them rather than just rolling around on the floor with them playing – they're learning as well.

(Emily)

Parents' responses to the question 'What is family learning?'

Reading with the children at home

Helping children with their homework

Doing things with the children – not just playing

Taking children on trips/outings

Friends helping out with the children

Discussing problems with other family members

It's also with other families – discussions of the problems you might have.

(Caroline)

Who is involved in family learning?

Once again, a group of parents was identified who have no partner or extended family members to call upon for participation in family learning. Other parents valued the input from their own parents.

Parents' responses to the question 'Who is involved in family learning?'

Just me and my kids
- I don't see any of my family
- they don't see their dad

Siblings

Grandparents

Social services

My children tend to go up to their nan's a lot at weekends. She sits down – she seems to have more patience with them and they really do come on.

(Caroline)

My dad helps with Julian – he loves sitting down and counting with him.

(Gloria)

I don't see any of my family so mine don't have that. It's just me and my kids.

(Emily)

Where does family learning take place?

These parents also recognised the wide spectrum of places in which family learning occurs.

**Parents' responses to the question
'Where does family learning take place?'**

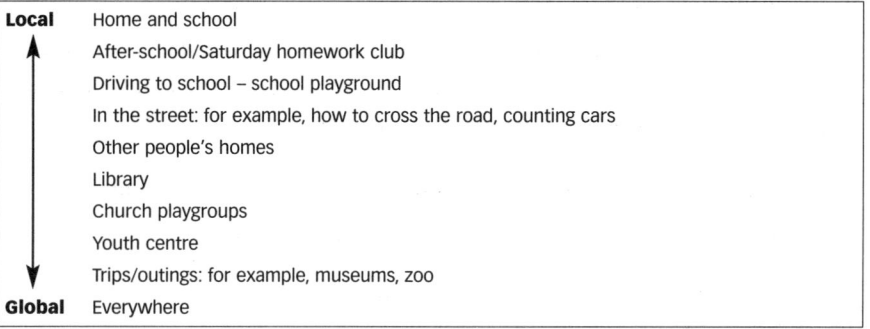

Even walking to school you're learning, 'What type of tree is that?'

(Caroline)

What involvement do you have in your child(ren)'s learning/education?

The involvement these parents reported in their children's education ranged from non-existent to fairly extensive.

Parents' responses to the question 'What involvement do you have in your child(ren)'s learning/education?'

None – I've never been asked to go to the school
Go along to the school and keep up to date
Parents' evenings
A lot – my child has special needs and I liaise closely with the teacher regarding her progress and homework

I'm always asking how they're getting on, coming to parents' evenings.

(Emily)

I have seen [my daughter's] teacher a couple of times, to ask how she's getting on and see if she's got any extra work, because she's special needs ... and she needs extra help with her reading, so the teacher puts things in her bag, letters, you know, so I can tell by that way.

(Caroline)

What motivates you to learn?

The things quoted by these parents as motivating them to learn were those with tangible gains or consequences. These parents were less likely to emphasise the personal emotional/spiritual reasons for wanting to learn.

Parents' responses to the question 'What motivates you to learn?'

Need to answer children's questions

To gain experience/qualification to progress in the workplace

Get something for yourself – own achievement

You get something from it. If you've got a job and you've been studying on a course or something and you want to do something, you try hard to get it and when you do get it, you get a job, or wherever you want to go, and go higher on the ladder.

(Caroline)

I didn't do sums at school – I wasn't allowed, so I never went to school. I don't really know that much about what they're doing. My oldest one is always saying, 'I know more than you.'

(Emily)

What are the barriers to learning?

It was primarily felt that lack of time due to childcare commitments and the costs of studying were the main barriers to learning. However, upon delving deeper, some of these parents admitted that it was something more personal that was preventing them from getting involved.

Parents' responses to the question 'What are the barriers to learning?'

Practical	Personal
Time	Laziness
Children and childcare	Previous bad experiences
Courses too long	Lack of will power
Financial costs	Fear of the unexpected and looking stupid

Some [courses] go on for years don't they, they drag. By the time you finish it you might realise you don't want to do that.

(Emily)

Who wants to go on courses? I hated school so I'm not going to want to go to college!

(Gloria)

It's the money as well though isn't it? You're paying for everything in your house, your rent, and by the time you've worked and paid all that, it's not worth even doing it really. You're better off [not studying].

(Emily)

Who might run a family learning course?

These parents believed that the council or social services probably funded family learning courses, which were delivered by teachers at schools and colleges. However, they said that such courses *should* be run by a parent, preferably one with whom they were already familiar.

With another parent; people can talk to other parents a lot easier, when it's someone they know – you can express yourself more. You hold things back when it's someone you don't know. It makes it easier if it's a parent or a friend. Someone you've been involved with before I suppose.

(Emily)

Parents' responses to the question 'Who might run a family learning course?'

Don't know
Someone you know
Another parent
Teachers
Schools
Colleges
Council
Social services

What might the subject matter of a family learning course be?

These parents seemed unaware of the numeracy and literacy courses that were currently on offer and they focused their ideas in this section on life/ social skills and computers. Although these are also topics of current family learning provision, it was notable that literacy and numeracy were omitted by these parents. It is possible that this omission may be related to their bad experiences at school, since these are the very topics they would have been taught during their childhood (as opposed to IT or parenting skills).

Parents' responses to the question 'What might the subject matter of a family learning course be?'

Pregnancy, childcare
What children are learning at school
Computers – IT
Social skills
Way of life – how to keep calm

I get quite stressed out when people don't believe me. Learning how to speak to your kids without shouting every five minutes. Getting them to listen to you as well instead of everything going in one ear and out the other.

(Emily)

What might be the benefits to you from you attending a family learning course?

Despite initially sounding quite wary of organised learning projects and courses, these parents could very clearly identify some of the benefits to getting involved in such an initiative. Like participating parents, they focused on both practical and personal issues.

Parents' responses to the question 'What might be the benefits to you from attending a family learning course?'

Practical	Personal
Gaining new knowledge	Pride at achievement and progress made – receiving a certificate/qualification
Experience/qualification resulting in better employment prospects and increased earnings – better quality of life	Becoming a better person
	Being part of a group – sharing experiences with other parents

> It makes you feel proud of what you've done, don't it, you've got something, you've achieved something to show for it.
>
> (Caroline)

> You'd be a changed person really, wouldn't you? You'd be out doing something you've never done before.
>
> (Emily)

> I'd communicate with [my daughter] better ... if I could learn the way she's learning I'd be able to sit down and communicate better with her.
>
> (Caroline)

What might be the benefits to your children from you attending a family learning course?

These parents focused less on the child's emotional and social gains and more on the practical and parental gains of participation.

Parents' responses to the question 'What might be the benefits to your children from you attending a family learning course?'

Practical	Parental
They learn new things	You have more to teach them
They are better prepared for school	You understand what they are being taught at school
	You communicate with children better

> Easier to understand what she's doing. It'd help a lot actually. She panics because I show her a different way to do things and it'd help stop that panic.
>
> (Caroline)

> My children aren't coming home with homework yet but it would be handy to be prepared, to be able to help my children at home.
>
> (Emily)

Who else might benefit from you attending a family learning course?

Like the participating parents, one of these parents felt that their participation in a family learning course might have an impact on everyone else they would encounter. The other parents conceived of benefits to others which related more directly to the information they might gain on a course.

Parents' responses to the question 'Who else might benefit from you attending a family learning course?'

Friends – relay information
People to whom you promote the course – they get involved
Whoever you communicate with – better social skills

> Whoever you communicate with really. You're passing on information that could help others. You could tell people you've been on a course and then they'd go and you're getting more people involved.
>
> (Caroline)

What might be the disadvantages to you from attending a family learning course?

Finances, travel and time were the major themes of comments supplied here.

Parents' responses to the question 'What might be the disadvantages to you from attending a family learning course?'

Travelling a long way
Travelling to an unfamiliar place
Financial costs of travel and enrolments/course fees
Having to organise/pay for childcare – relying on others
Children giving away information about your family life to alternative carers
Time spent neglecting other commitments

Depends where you've got to go for it and the money to get there and who can have the kids while you're there, because obviously I've got no family near me or anyone … I keep getting letters from the Job Centre now that [my daughter] is four saying, 'Are you looking for work?' and all this lot, 'We'll help you, you'll be benefiting from all this extra money,' but you don't get any extra money really, do you? They're not going to pay for childcare or things like that, which we can't afford.

(Emily)

What might be the disadvantages to your child(ren) from you attending a course?

The issues which parents raised here focused on the absence encountered through being parted from their child.

Mine tend to play up when there's strangers around, they get a bit showing off, try and go so far with them, see how far they can get. I'd be too scared to leave mine with strangers.

(Emily)

Parents' responses to the question 'What might be the disadvantages to your child(ren) from you attending a course?'

Leaving them with strangers
They'd see less of you than they were used to

What might be the disadvantages to others from you attending a course?

These parents could not identify a single disadvantage to others as a result of their hypothesised attendance on a course.

What about a family learning course would make it successful?

Parents were very clear that success depended on familiarity with the teacher and fellow students, as well as the course content being easy enough to understand and interesting. They were also very concerned about help with, or care for, their younger children.

Parents' reponses to the question 'What about a family learning course would make it successful?'

Timed to fit in with childcare responsibilities
Helpers to look after younger children
Small numbers of students
Being with people you know – not with strangers
Being given a choice
Getting clear information about what to expect
Content delivered at the appropriate level of understanding
Content that is relevant and interesting
Provided with a clear goal or objective

Give us a choice, talk us through it. I've got no confidence so I couldn't just walk into a college and do all that. It'd be easier wouldn't it, a couple of us going that know each other.

(Emily)

I find it really hard to sit around a big table of people.

(Rebecca)

If you could find out more about the course before you went on it, it would be better, more information.

(Caroline)

What family learning courses, if any, would you like to attend?

Although all of these parents had not considered previously attending a family learning course, when asked, two decided that they might. The other two parents could not think of a particular course they would attend but it was clear that the focus group discussion had sparked their interest in this issue.

Parents' responses to the question 'What family learning courses, if any, would you like to attend?'

I haven't really thought about it
Don't know yet but I think it's important
Childcare
Computers

I haven't really thought about it ... with five [children]!

(Gloria)

I want to go and learn computers because all the offices today are run by computers and I haven't got a clue. All I know is how to turn them on and how to turn them off.

(Caroline)

What would prevent you from attending a course?

The issues raised in this section echoed some of the reasons reported as barriers to learning, thus acting as an internal consistency check on the parents' reported attitudes. Once again, their comments could be divided into personal issues, practical issues and course-related issues.

Parents' responses to the question 'What would prevent you from attending a course?'

Personal	Practical	Course-related
Shyness	Children and childcare	Feeling the courses are • inconsistent – changing teachers
Fear of large groups of strangers strangers	Money	• too short with no support, feed-back or follow-up • authoritative – you're told what to do
Lack of confidence		
		Perception that it's hard work
		Bureaucracy – involvement of social services

It's just nerves I think, having the courage to get up and learn and let someone else tell you what to do again ... It's hard work! ... It makes you look stupid, don't it?

(Emily)

My partner works full time from the early hours to late at night.

(Rebecca)

People are scared of social services really, aren't they? You don't want to keep getting them involved in your family life. You just get rid of them and then you get told, 'Well, you can have this if they refer you,' and I'm thinking, no, I don't want to go through all of that again!

(Emily)

You get used to one person doing these courses, don't you, and a couple of weeks later there's another person. It's never just one person you can sit down and get on with.

(Rebecca)

How might you encourage people to attend?

Like the participating parents, these parents were keen to encourage attendance through word of mouth. They too felt that it was not necessary to alter the actual course content, but rather the message of what the course contained. Again, the topic of the course was not mentioned as a something which could be altered to encourage wider participation.

Parents' responses to the question 'How might you encourage people to attend?'

> Change their names – not 'Mother and Child', rather 'Parent and Child'
>
> Change message of what course is about, rather than course itself
>
> Tell others what you've learnt
> • emphasise the fun
> • emphasise communication you've had with your child

Just tell them how much fun you've had, how much communication you've had with [the children].

(Caroline)

There's a lot of dads that do come in to pick their kids up from school, a lot of them, but there's nothing aimed at just dads.

(Emily)

Other comments

After a certain amount of initial suspicion and scepticism, these very disadvantaged women were drawn into a very expressive discussion of what family learning might look like to them which left them feeling that, after they had probed their own feelings, it was in fact an important issue. The lasting impression formed was one of their need to be coaxed and encouraged to participate, with promises of adequate support and follow-up.

Parents' other comments

> We should be encouraged more to participate
>
> Information should be clearer and more simple

Sometimes there's words in [letters home from school] that you think, what?!

(Caroline)

Chapter 5

Overview of the Research

In response to a request from the Department for Education and Skills (DfES) (in its former guise as the Department for Education and Employment, or DfEE), a three-month qualitative research project was undertaken to investigate family learning. The objective of this research was to obtain parents' perspectives on what family learning might look like to them, what their expectations of it might be, how they would want it to happen and where, what they might get out of it and the right way of describing it from their point of view, i.e. a bottom-up approach.

In order to meet this objective, a series of focus group discussions both with parents who were participating and who were not participating in organised family learning initiatives were carried out. The research collected the views of parents involved in six different family learning courses (at nursery and primary schools and a secondary school), four of which were numeracy courses and two of which were literacy courses. In each of these, parents spent time learning with their children as well spending time learning on their own. These parents came from a broad range of family structures and ethnic and educational backgrounds. Two of the discussions were carried out in one London borough and the remaining discussions and interviews were carried out in a second London borough.

The research findings summarised below are based upon five focus group discussions with a total of 25 family learning course participants, two in-depth interviews with family learning course participants, and one focus group discussion with four non-participating parents. In total, 31 parents were consulted.

'Participating' parents

Learning was conceptualised as anything from something very formal and structured in an educational setting to something far less structured and more informal taking place in almost all of everyday life.

Learning was seen both practically, as a means to an end – to gain a qualification to help get a good job – and as something fun and expressive which could result in enhanced self-awareness.

Family learning was conceptualised as anything from parents playing with their children at home and helping them with homework, to understanding what children do in school, to getting all of the family involved in helping with children. Many parents reiterated the philosophy of adult education, agreeing that family learning was about adults learning too.

Family learning usually involves parents, children, grandparents, god-parents and friends. In some instances it was seen as including people on television, people in the street and health professionals. In some circumstances, such a wide support network does not exist and family learning only takes place between mothers and their children.

Family learning was widely recognised as taking place everywhere, including the home, the street, health centres, after-school clubs, and outings to the zoo or seaside.

Motivation to learn was either to do something for oneself or to do something for one's children. In relation to themselves, parents were motivated to gain qualifications, improve their employment situation, be more stimulated, have contact with others or gain more confidence. In relation to their children, parents were motivated to be able to teach them more, prepare them for their future, do more for their children than their own parents had for them and better understand the education system.

Things which might prevent parents from learning included practical issues such as time and lack of physical and financial support for childcare; personal issues such as low confidence and lack of will power; course-related issues such as poor accessibility and poor availability; and issues related to other people, such as negative attitudes and a lack of emotional support.

The benefits that parents identified relating to their participation in a family learning course could be divided into four areas: (1) child-related – where they became more aware of how to teach their children and the opportunities available to do so in everyday life; (2) 'other-related' – where parents gained from meeting new people, making friends and developing a new support network; (3) practical – where they gained new knowledge and were awarded a certificate, which motivated them to want to progress to other courses; and (4) emotional – where parents felt they were discovering their 'old selves', reawakening their brains and gaining more confidence.

> I quite like ... playing a small part of Kathryn's nursery because she says to me, 'Oh is it a numeracy day today?' – she likes the fact that I'm here ... You're seeing them in this environment, where, I think, they change. They're really independent; it's really exciting for parents to see your child thriving like that without you and just to see how they learn and ask other people questions. Plus, I actually like coming in and doing activities here because you feel a part of the whole learning process that they're experiencing.
>
> (Chullaki)

Clear benefits were also recognised in relation to the children that took part in the course. These included improved reading, improved vocabulary, improved concentration, better relationships with other children and adults, increased confidence and more respect for their parents as better role models.

> The one-to-one interaction is great because I don't get a lot of time to give him the time and attention that he needs – it's just one-to-one for a solid hour, trying to absorb it all ... I can see my son's definitely

learning from it, I mean, once a day he'll pick up on something he learnt in the group ... So it pushes me to carry on with it because I can see he's really benefiting from it, really gaining.

(Ellen)

Others who were thought to benefit as a result of parents attending the course included: other members of the family to whom course information could be passed; future educators who would benefit from more able children; and everyone that the parents might communicate with as a result of their enhanced self-esteem and improved social skills. Some had a very global view, in that they felt all of society would benefit.

The reasons given for the course being successful could be divided into three areas: (1) the practical organisation of the course, for example, the free crèche for younger children, the diversity of topics studied, the flexibility of what to study, the small numbers of students, and the friendly and informal atmosphere; (2) the other people attending the course, who were friendly, non-judgemental and keen to learn; and (3) the teacher, who was supportive, encouraging, non-intimidating and respectful.

Very few disadvantages of attending the course could be identified, but those that were mentioned included: a lack of time to complete all units of the course; worry that when it ended there would be a void to fill; the disruption caused to the children being removed and returned to normal classes; and having to leave other children with other carers.

Many parents said that they would like to take part in another family learning course, some were planning to enrol in more formal courses at college and some felt that this had been the start of their pathway back to work.

When asked how others might be encouraged to attend, these parents emphasised the need to provide clear and simple information about what to expect, that the benefits to the children should be emphasised, that open days should be promoted and that talking to parents who had already been on the course would help. They did not suggest altered course content, which is interesting given that, for example, men might be more likely to attend a course with a more practical or physical focus.

Thus the overall feeling was incredibly positive, with all participants having enjoyed their course very much indeed. The following quote demonstrates just what impact attending such a course can have:

I already know my brain is starting to wake up and I feel a better person for it. By doing something like this it's made me feel more like my old self, the person I like being. It's already making me feel ready to be capable enough of branching off into doing other courses ... given me more self-confidence, motivation big time. It's also a release from my day-to-day normal living, you know, it's like a little social gathering as well ... it's important to me, it has done a lot for me ... I'm starting to get a direction in life.

(Tina)

'Non-participating' parents

Learning for these parents was also construed in formal, practical terms – gaining a qualification to get a good job – as well as in more informal terms: life in general.

Family learning was similarly conceptualised as helping children at home with their homework and taking them on outings, as well as discussing problems with other family members. Again, a whole host of people were recognised as taking part in family learning, especially grandparents, and examples of lone mothers without any support network were again uncovered, demonstrating that in these cases family learning could only involve the mother and her children.

Family learning was again recognised as taking place everywhere, including the home, the street, museums, youth centres and libraries.

Motivation to learn was also split into doing something for oneself (practical or emotional/personal) and doing something for one's children.

The things cited as barriers to involvement in learning for this group were previous bad experiences of learning, lack of time, lack of will power, laziness and the financial costs of childcare and course attendance.

Who wants to go on courses? I hated school so I'm not going to want to go to college!

(Gloria)

When asked to conceptualise what a family learning course might be about or who might run it and where, these parents came up with ideas not dissimilar to the provision currently on offer – for example, parenting skills or computer courses run by the council at schools. It was notable that they did not describe literacy or numeracy courses, the very topics which they would have been taught at school. They also thought that social services might run courses and, although they felt that these courses were probably being delivered in formal educational settings, they felt strongly that they should take place in informal settings and be 'taught' by another parent or a friend – someone with whom they were familiar.

This group had a clear sense that there could be benefits to both themselves and their children from attending a family learning course. Like those cited by participating parents, these advantages included practical issues such as acquiring new knowledge and skills, as well as personal issues such as pride in achievement and improved communication skills. They also felt that others would benefit from them relaying the course information.

> My children aren't coming home with homework yet but it would be handy to be prepared, to be able to help my children at home.
>
> (Emily)

Disadvantages of attending a course that were cited included: travelling a long way to an unfamiliar place; the costs involved; and time spent neglecting other commitments. These parents seemed to be unaware that such courses might be run within their community during school hours, with free childcare provision for their younger children.

When asked how a family learning course should be designed to make it a success these parents stated that it should involve small numbers of people they knew; it should be delivered at the appropriate level; the content should be clear, interesting and relevant; and on-site childcare should be provided.

This group felt that people might be encouraged to attend a family learning course if they heard directly from other parents who had already been on the course. They also felt that there should be a change to the message of what each course was about, rather than to the course itself – in other words, clearer, more simple information about the courses. Although a couple of these parents had not given any thought to attending a family learning course prior to the discussion, all were left stating that they were going to investigate what was available in their area.

After a certain amount of initial scepticism, these parents concluded that family learning was in fact an important issue. The lasting impression formed was one of their need to be coaxed and encouraged to participate, with promises of adequate support and follow-up. This feeling is reflected by 'Emily':

> Give us a choice, talk us through it. I've got no confidence so I couldn't just walk into a college and do all that. It'd be easier, wouldn't it, a couple of us going that know each other.
>
> (Emily)

Chapter 6

Discussion and Recommendations

SUMMARY OF FINDINGS

The comments made by all of the parents interviewed were remarkably consistent across age, ethnic groups and marital status, and, where relevant, across type of course, age of child attending course and course location. There was a very small effect of educational attainment on the comments of some of the participating parents, yet due to the small numbers involved it would be difficult to draw any conclusions about this without further investigation. Further research would need to be carried out on a larger sample to ascertain whether this consistency is real or an artefact of this small-scale project.

It is clear that the overall impression formed by the parents participating in family learning initiatives was a positive one. All of them had enjoyed their course and could see a large number of benefits to themselves, to their children and to others from attending. These benefits ranged from practical and tangible gains (a certificate of achievement, improved vocabulary of child) to emotional and psychological gains (rediscovery of 'old' self, increased confidence in themselves and their children). The comments from teachers and pupils at one centre also add further weight to these benefits, validating the opinions of the parents involved. The benefits cited by participating parents were closely tied to their motivations to learn and, in this sense, one might say that their pursuit of learning had the desired effect.

Both participating and non-participating parents were clear that learning and family learning could be carried out almost anywhere and by a wide range of people, most especially themselves, their children and their children's grandparents. However, there was a group of parents who had no partner or extended family to call upon to take part in family learning. These parents felt very much that it was just them and their child(ren) who could be involved.

The reasons that non-participating parents quoted for not participating in (family) learning related to their previous bad experiences of learning at school. They were also very cognisant of the fact that they lacked the will power to get involved in something more organised, and also expressed some concern at attending a course in a formal educational setting where they would be with a large group of strangers in front of whom they might look stupid. When they spoke of time, distance and the financial costs of childcare as additional barriers to learning, they seemed to be unaware of the existence of courses that were actually being run in their community in less formal settings with free crèche facilities. This probably says something about the way in which those courses were being promoted or advertised; these parents recognised that they were more likely to get involved in such initiatives if they heard from other parents who had been involved, as opposed to receiving wordy letters from the school. After a certain amount of initial scepticism, the non-participating parents concluded that family learning was in fact an important issue, although it was clear that they would need to be coaxed and encouraged to participate in these courses, with promises of adequate support and follow-up.

RESEARCH CAVEATS

So, what can this research tell us about how family learning courses should be organised in the future? Perhaps we should first turn our attention to some of the shortcomings of this research before proceeding with a discussion of suggestions for future research. The first of these is that data collection was focused mainly on those people who were involved, or had been involved, in a family learning course. This was in recognition that there may be some parents who find it difficult to grasp the concept of family learning and imagine and convey their ideal scenario (especially those who are less confident, less articulate and less educated, i.e. precisely those we might expect to benefit most from attending such a course). However, one could argue that since a group of non-participating parents was interviewed, the members of whom provided a wealth of very articulate information concerning their views of family learning and reasons for non-participation, the findings have been balanced somewhat. The group of non-participating parents was also a group of women who were very disadvantaged; precisely those that one might expect could benefit greatly from involvement in a family learning initiative and whose opinions were thus invaluable.

All but one of the participants was female, which could have introduced a heavy gender bias to the views reported. Although it was clear that these courses were mainly attended by mothers, it was apparent that a couple of fathers did attend some of the groups; however, on the days that the focus group discussions were carried out only one father had attended. While one might assume that males are less likely to talk emotionally and personally about the subject of family learning and might have stayed away from the course intentionally on the day that they anticipated a researcher arriving, most parents did not seem to be aware of the research discussion prior to the researcher's arrival and thus it was merely a matter of circumstance that only one father was interviewed.

Another thing to consider when reviewing the research findings of the participant parents is that their comments all relate to literacy or numeracy courses, which they attended during the day. This project did not therefore gather views of those attending other types of family learning courses (e.g. arts, crafts, DIY, sports, parenting skills, IT, music, drama and theatre, languages) or those run in the evenings, which might attract a higher male attendance as well as those in full-time work. Thus the views collected were those of a largely female non-working population. In addition, all of the courses attended were based in London, which could introduce a geographical bias to the results.

One should also be aware that a positive skew to the results might be expected owing to the fact that teachers on the courses volunteered to have their parents interviewed and, as such, the interviews may have only been conducted with those on successful courses; it is unlikely that teachers of courses that were less successful would have volunteered for participation in this research. In addition, the parents on these courses were 'self-selecting' and one could assume that these are the types of people who are more interested in their children's education, which would also give a positive skew to the results. However, the group of non-participating parents interviewed proved to be a useful corrective.

The research could also be criticised for being very short and small scale, providing only a snapshot of the views of a handful of parents in relation to these issues, and it is absolutely true that one cannot and should not generalise these findings to the population at large. However, one should not underestimate the value of qualitative research such as this, whose main aim is to unpack the issues and themes surrounding a particular subject with a group of people from diverse backgrounds and wide-ranging experiences. Indeed, research such as this can be used to inform further qualitative research and/or the design of larger-scale projects of a more quantitative nature.

RECOMMENDATIONS

Given these points, however, we can conclude that the results from the parents interviewed show that family learning courses had been (or would be) successful if they addressed three main areas:

1) Practical issues – courses should be free, be organised and explained clearly and simply, be easily accessed, offer a choice of content, be tailored to suit the individual, take place in an informal friendly atmosphere, offer free on-site childcare, and provide adequate follow-up and support with progression routes.

2) Issues relating to other 'students' – other students (parents) should be known or familiar, non-judgmental, keen to learn, work as a team, and have things in common.

3) Issues relating to the teacher – the teacher should be supportive and encouraging, non-intimidating and respectful, recognise individuals' capabilities, have a good approach to the children, also be a parent, and never act superior to the students.

This, in association with the recommendations made from participating parents as to how their course could have been improved, as well as the general parental perspectives uncovered in this research, have formed the basis for the following tentative recommendations about the future design and delivery of successful family learning literacy and numeracy initiatives.

Marketing

Family learning courses should be advertised in a way that emphasises that classes will not be reminiscent of parents' early formal education.

In promoting classes, organisations should avoid wordy letters sent home with children. They should concentrate on colourful posters which emphasise the benefits to children.

Organisations running family learning courses should also consider open days for parents to come in and observe a class in practice. They should encourage parents who have already been on the courses to talk to other parents about their experiences, emphasising that they were taught how to teach their children, made aware of the current education system, and benefited from the quality time they spent with their children and making new friends.

Organisations should encourage parents to enrol with a friend or promote the fact that friends can be made if they get involved.

Course structure

Family learning courses should be free.

The information about the courses should be clear and simple.

Courses should be easily accessed (located in the community), and widely available.

Courses should take place in an informal friendly atmosphere.

Free on-site childcare should be made available.

Courses should start late enough in the morning to allow parents time to complete all child and household-related responsibilities – for example, dropping children off at various locations. Although not raised by the parents consulted during this research, it is worth recommending that the timing of courses should also enable those in full-time work to attend: for instance, through the provision of family learning in the workplace.

Courses should run in tandem with standard educational terms, in order to cover more content/topics and ensure participants' interest is maintained by shorter gaps between courses or levels within courses.

Adequate follow-up and support should be provided, along with clear routes of progression.

Courses should offer a choice of content and be flexible (tailored to suit the individual). Again, the authors recommend that courses with a more practical or physical focus might attract more male participants.

Individual courses should cover a diversity of topics to ensure that they are engaging and interesting.

Ways should be devised for parents to work with their children in joint sessions which result in the least disruption to their child's usual routine and which do not remove their child from other valuable lessons.

Courses should provide parents with an overview of the course so that they know what will be covered each week, to allow preparation.

The 'students' (parents) on the courses should be small in number and known or familiar. They should also have things in common – be of a similar age group, be of the same gender, be of a similar educational attainment.

Teachers

Family learning course teachers should be trained to teach adults. This will result in them being supportive, encouraging, non-intimidating, respectful and non-patronising. They should not act as if superior to their students and they should not interrogate students when they miss a class. They should facilitate the 'catching-up' of missed material. (The authors recognise that many family learning courses are already taught by school teachers or adult tutors; this point aims to highlight this training requirement as a necessity for all. The authors also recognise that these practices would also be very much appreciated by all learners, regardless of age.)

Course teachers should be experienced and able to recognise individuals' capabilities.

Course teachers should be capable of dealing with children of all ages and abilities, and preferably be a parent themselves.

Course teachers should encourage students to be non-judgmental, keen to learn and work as a team.

CONCLUDING REMARKS

The results of this research reiterate the findings in the Ofsted report (Ofsted, 2000), which states that models of family learning are more successful at attracting participants from disadvantaged and under-represented groups where the curriculum is broad. Their report also recognises that family learning practitioners are very dedicated, thus identifying the qualities required to make a successful family learning teacher. One could assume that their dedication is a product of the fact that they can see how effective family learning is for those who participate, and this was certainly a feeling expressed by all of the teachers during the course of this research project. The parents interviewed certainly had a clear idea that family learning teachers were quite different to those they'd experienced at school, which for them was a positive thing, and they felt that such teachers should have qualities that allow them to relate to adults in a non-patronising way. Unfortunately, this research did not gather information on the training or qualifications of the teachers providing the courses, however, the parents' comments obviously have implications for the training of these tutors.

With regard to future research, more qualitative research could be conducted involving different types of non-participants (for example, those in full-time work), participating and non-participating males, those who attend evening courses, those who attend courses addressing subjects other than literacy and numeracy, and, as is evident from the preceding point, family learning teachers themselves. Indeed, following this, in order to make sound objective evidence-based recommendations for how family learning should be organised in the future, it would be necessary to undertake a longer-term quantitative piece of research, informed by the issues raised in the qualitative research, on a far larger sample size in a far wider range of locations and courses.

Finally, most documents about family learning emphasise the need for a clear policy (Buffton, 1999; Campaign for Learning, 2001); this document is no exception. Family learning initiatives would benefit from better planning at the centre and longer-term funding. These would promote more even, equitable and responsive provision.

APPENDIX 1.1 Email Sent to Numeracy Co-ordinator in London Borough 1

From: Angela Brassett-Grundy [abg@cls.ioe.ac.uk]
Sent: Monday, February 12, 2001 7:37 PM
To: Xxx Xxxx
Subject: Family Learning Research

Dear Xxx,

I am writing to you to see if you can give me some help or advice.

I am a research officer at the University of London's Institute of Education, and I am carrying out a piece of research for the DfEE into "Family Learning". For this, I need to organise some focus groups so that I can talk to [London borough 1] residents about their ideas and experiences of family learning. I need to recruit people who are attending (or have attended) organised programmes or initiatives that help them develop their own skills, enhance their understanding of their children's education, as well as develop their parenting skills. These can be people who have participated in learning initiatives alongside their children, or those who have participated in initiatives which they attended on their own. In addition, I also need to talk to some parents who have not attended any formal organised family learning programmes, particularly those for whom such initiatives would be extremely beneficial.

As you are the family numeracy consultant for the [London borough 1] Numeracy Project, I wondered whether you had any ideas of how I can get in touch with parents in [London borough 1] to recruit to the focus groups I have described? Do you know which schools/colleges/community centres have delivered such programmes? If so, could I contact the head teachers/principals/managers in question to ask them if I could speak to the parents who attend? Is there a way in which you could contact parents on my behalf?

The timescale is very short indeed - I need to organise these groups for late February/early March. Any ideas that you have would be greatly appreciated!

Thank you in anticipation of your help,

Yours sincerely,

Angela Brassett-Grundy

Angela Brassett-Grundy,
Research Officer,
Centre for Longitudinal Studies,
University of London Institute of Education,
6th Floor, 20 Bedford Way,
London WC1H 0AL

Tel. No.: 020 7612 6876
Email Address: abg@cls.ioe.ac.uk

APPENDIX 2.1 Email Sent to Lifelong Learning Co-ordinator in London Borough 2

From: Angela Brassett-Grundy [abg@cls.ioe.ac.uk]
Sent: Tuesday, February 13, 2001 12:29 PM
To: Xxx Xxxx
Subject: Family Learning Research

Dear Xxx,

Following our conversation this morning, I have written a letter giving you more information about the research, which I have attached as a Word file. Let me know if you have problems opening it and I'll send it in a different format.

Thank you for your help.

Regards,

Angela

Angela Brassett-Grundy,
Research Officer,
Centre for Longitudinal Studies,
University of London Institute of Education,
6th Floor, 20 Bedford Way,
London. WC1H 0AL

Tel. No.: 020 7612 6876
Email Address: abg@cls.ioe.ac.uk

The letter attached to this email can be seen in Appendix 2.2.

APPENDIX 2.2 Letter Attached to Email Sent to Lifelong Learning Co-ordinator in London Borough 2

Centre for Longitudinal Studies

Director Professor John Bynner
Deputy Director Professor Heather Joshi
Telephone 020 7612 6900
Fax 020 7612 6880
Email cls@slc.ioe.ac.uk
Website www.cls.ioe.ac.uk

INSTITUTE OF EDUCATION
20 BEDFORD WAY
LONDON WC1H 0AL
Telephone 020 7612 6900
Fax 020 7612 6880
Website www.ioe.ac.uk

Director Professor Geoff Whitty

By e-mail to:
Xxx Xxxx
Lifelong Learning Co-ordinator
[London borough 2] Local Educational Authority
<email address>

13th February, 2001

Dear Xxx,

Re: Family Learning Research

Thank you for taking the time to chat to me this morning about a piece of research I am working on for the Department for Education and Employment. As requested, I am writing to let you know in more detail what the project involves.

I have been asked to carry out a piece of qualitative research investigating people's experiences of family learning, through focus groups. I am keen to find out what people's views of family learning are, what their personal experiences have been, and what they consider are the good and bad points of various initiatives they have been involved in. Thus, I aim to set up four focus groups, each with six participants. Two of the focus groups will consist of people who *have* been involved in an organised family learning project/initiative and two focus groups will consist of people with *no* experience of formalised family learning.

As the lifelong learning coordinator within the [London borough 2] LEA, I understand that you have access to a team of people that lead various formalised family learning/parent education projects around [London borough 2]. I wondered whether you would invite them to promote this piece of research to the people and parents involved in their projects, to see if any of them would be prepared to participate in one of the focus groups. I would also appreciate it if you could advise me or help put me in touch with people who have not participated in any of your projects, who would be willing to take part in one of my 'inexperienced' groups. I am open to your suggestions and advice on how to contact such people and appreciate the fact that their having chosen not to participate in one of your initiatives may make it unlikely that they'll want to participate in my research!

Each focus group discussion will last approximately one and a half hours long. It will take place at a location that is most convenient for the participants to get to, and one in which they feel most comfortable (e.g. one of the family learning project venues). Again, the timing of the discussion will be arranged purely for the convenience of the parents, and each person will be reimbursed any costs incurred in attending (I am trying to ensure that some payment could be given to participants but am waiting for authorisation). Perhaps it goes without saying that refreshments will also be provided. All of the participants' comments will remain confidential and shall be anonymised when incorporated into my reports.

My timetable is very short in that I hope to run the focus groups by early March at the latest but given that I live in [London borough 2] I can come and visit you, and any of your colleagues, at very short notice indeed. I am available all day Mondays and Tuesdays, up until 3 p.m. on Wednesdays and Fridays, and on Thursdays before 12 p.m. I don't know if you work Saturdays but I can easily come along any time then too.

I hope that this gives you a better idea of the research I hope to carry out. I would like to emphasise that your co-operation will be fully acknowledged in my final report to the DfEE and that I will also prepare a report of my findings specifically for your information. I will also write a newsletter-style summary of my findings to send to each focus group participant.

Thank you very much for your co-operation. I look forward to hearing from you soon.

Yours sincerely,

ANGELA BRASSETT-GRUNDY
Research Officer

Tel No: 020 7612 6876
Email: abg@cls.ioe.ac.uk

APPENDIX 3.1 Flyer/Poster Designed to Encourage Parents to Participate in the Research

Earn £10! Earn £10! Earn £10! Earn £10! Earn £10! Earn £10! Earn £10!

<u>Family Learning Research</u>

Would you like to contribute to a very important piece of government-funded research by participating in a small group discussion concerning your experiences of learning, 'family learning' and/or 'shared learning'? If so, read on ...

I work at the Institute of Education at London University, and I am carrying out a piece of research that will form part of a report to government. As a result, I am looking for parents who have been involved (or are currently involved) in a family/shared learning project, to take part in a group discussion concerning the type of project they were involved in and what they thought about it:

- Perhaps the project helped you with reading, writing or computer skills?
- Perhaps the project helped you to help your children with their schoolwork?
- Perhaps you and your child learnt something together?

Whatever your experience is, I would love to hear from you.

The discussion will involve up to eight parents talking in a group about their learning experiences. It will last about 1½ hours, and will take place towards the end of February or early March, at a time and place that is most convenient for the volunteers. Everything that you discuss will remain **completely confidential**!

I would like to hear from you, whether you are a mother or a father, and whatever your age, religion or ethnic origin is – everyone's opinion counts and everyone has something valuable to say about their experiences!

If you would like **your views** represented to the government's Department for Education and Employment, whilst earning yourself **£10** in the process, please contact me using any of the methods below. If you want to find out more before you decide whether to participate, please feel free to call me for a chat any time.

Thank you for your time – I look forward to hearing from you soon!

Postal Address:	Angela Brassett-Grundy, Research Officer, Centre for Longitudinal Studies, Institute of Education – University of London, 6th Floor, 20 Bedford Way, London. WC1H 0AL
Email Address:	abg@cls.ioe.ac.uk
Tel No:	020 7612 6876

APPENDIX 4.1 Focus Group Topic Guide – 'Participants'

GOAL/INTRODUCTION

Family learning is one of the critical elements of lifelong learning, the broader view of which encompasses intergenerational learning, parental involvement in children's education, and parenting skills.

The goal of this research is to obtain the perspective of families on what family learning might look like to them: what their expectations of it might be; how they would want it to happen and where; what they might get out of it; and, what is the right way of describing it from their point of view.

This guide is to be used with people who HAVE been involved in an organised family learning programme/initiative.

INTRODUCTION – LEARNING IN GENERAL

What are your feelings about learning?
What does learning mean to you?

How do you motivate yourself to learn?
How do you motivate your child(ren) to learn?
If you are not motivated to learn, why?

What are the barriers to (being motivated to) learn?
What kind of involvement do you have in your child(ren)'s education?

PROGRAMME PARTICIPATION – DESCRIPTION

Describe the programme/initiative you were involved in.

Prompts
- location
- timing
- frequency
- overall duration

- members of own family present
- other participants (age groups, numbers, roles)
- provider(s) (multi-agency collaboration?)
- subject matter
  - ➤ improving child's skills
  - ➤ improving parenting skills
  - ➤ improving own skills
- formality – open/closed/drop-in
- assessment methods (self-assessment, practical exercises, psychometric tests, other tests, referral)
- delivery mode – small groups, workbooks, ICT, combinations.

BENEFITS OF FAMILY LEARNING

What were the benefits/advantages of the programme to you?

Prompts
- knowledge of/competency in particular subject
- qualifications
- progression to other courses/training/better jobs
- knowledge of child development
- better relationships with children
- better contact with schools
- increased confidence/esteem.

What were the benefits/advantages of the programme to your child(ren)?

Prompts
- accelerated development, e.g. pre-school oral skills
- improved existing skills, e.g. in literacy and numeracy
- increased confidence/esteem
- improved health
- improved behaviour – positive attitudes
- pleasure in learning – normal adult activity too.

What benefits were there to other people?

Prompts
- other members of your family – relationships, support, communication
- your community – relationships, support, communication.

What was it about the programme that brought about these benefits? What made it made it successful?

Prompts
- location
- timing
- frequency
- overall duration
- members of own family present
- other participants (age-groups, numbers, roles)
- provider(s) (multi-agency collaboration?)
- subject matter
  - ➤ improving child's skills
  - ➤ improving parenting skills
  - ➤ improving own skills
- formality – open/closed/drop-in
- assessment methods (self-assessment, practical exercises, psychometric tests, other tests, referral)
- delivery mode – small groups, workbooks, ICT, combinations.

COSTS OF FAMILY LEARNING

What were the drawbacks/disadvantages of the programme to you?

Prompts
- teacher unable to cope with disparate needs of two groups
- different teachers with different approaches
- poorly planned – no focus or clear objective
- lack of formal assessment
- lack of support
- curriculum too narrow
- appealed to one type of person or a specific section of community.

What were the drawbacks/disadvantages of the programme to your child(ren)?

Prompts
- teacher unable to cope with disparate needs of two groups
- different teachers with different approaches
- poorly planned – no focus or clear objective
- lack of formal assessment
- lack of support
- curriculum too narrow
- withdrawn from important school lessons to participate
- targeted at inappropriate level – too easy/hard so no progress made.

What drawbacks or disadvantages were there to other people?

Prompts
- other members of your family – relationships, support, communication
- your community – relationships, support, communication.

What was it about the programme that brought about these drawbacks/disadvantages? What made it unsuccessful?

Prompts
- location
- timing
- frequency
- overall duration
- members of own family present
- other participants (age groups, numbers, roles)
- provider(s) (multi-agency collaboration?)
- subject matter
  - ➤ improving child's skills
  - ➤ improving parenting skills
  - ➤ improving own skills
- formality – open/closed/drop-in
- assessment methods (self-assessment, practical exercises, psychometric tests, other tests, referral)
- delivery mode – small groups, workbooks, ICT, combinations.

How could the programme have been improved?

Prompts
- location
- timing
- frequency
- overall duration
- members of own family present
- other participants (age groups, numbers, roles)
- provider(s) (multi-agency collaboration?)
- subject matter
  - ➤ improving child's skills
  - ➤ improving parenting skills
  - ➤ improving own skills
- formality – open/closed/drop-in
- assessment methods (self-assessment, practical exercises, psychometric tests, other tests, referral)
- delivery mode – small groups, workbooks, ICT, combinations

PARTICIPATION IN FAMILY LEARNING

Can you think of other types of programme that would have worked as well, or that you would have liked to participate in? Describe them.

Prompts
- different subject matter
  - ➤ literacy
  - ➤ numeracy
  - ➤ ICT
  - ➤ arts and crafts
  - ➤ sports
  - ➤ languages
  - ➤ therapeutic
  - ➤ music
- different timing/location etc.

What other types of family learning would you take part in, ideally, in the future?

How could other people be encouraged to participate in these programmes?
- men
- ethnic minorities
- most disadvantaged/poorest skilled families.

CLOSING COMMENTS

Is there anything you would like to add about your feelings concerning family learning?

Is there anything else you would like to say in relation to the things we have been discussing?

APPENDIX 4.2 Focus Group Topic Guide – 'Non-Participants'

GOAL/INTRODUCTION

Family learning is one of the critical elements of lifelong learning, the broader view of which encompasses intergenerational learning, parental involvement in children's education, and parenting skills.

The goal of this research is to obtain the perspective of families on what family learning might look like to them: what their expectations of it might be; how they would want it to happen and where; what they might get out of it; and, what is the right way of describing it from their point of view.

This guide is to be used with people who have NOT been involved in an organised family learning programme/initiative.

INTRODUCTION – LEARNING IN GENERAL

What are your feelings about learning?
What does learning mean to you?

How do you motivate yourself to learn?
How do you motivate your child(ren) to learn?
If you are not motivated to learn, why?

What are the barriers to (being motivated to) learn?
What kind of involvement do you have in your child(ren)'s education?

WHAT IS FAMILY LEARNING?

What do you think of when you hear the words 'family learning'?

What is your idea of family learning?

Who takes part in family learning?

Prompts

- children alone
- parents alone
- children and parents
- grandparents
- older siblings
- other family members.

Where could/does family learning take place?

Prompts

- the family itself
- schools/colleges/training centres
- libraries
- community centres
- youth centres
- museums/galleries/arts centres
- leisure centres
- religious institutions.

Who would run an organised family learning programme/initiative?

Prompts

- education services
- teachers/trainers
- local authority
- health visitors
- health services
- other health professionals
- voluntary organisations
- community/youth leaders
- religious organisations
- religious leaders.

What would the subject matter of the programme be?

Prompts
- children's skills – literary/numeracy/IT/arts and crafts/sports
- parenting skills
- parent's skills – literary/numeracy/IT/ arts and crafts/sports.

BENEFITS OF FAMILY LEARNING

What do you think the benefits of family learning might be for you?

Prompts
- knowledge of/competency in particular subject
- qualifications, progression to other courses/training/better jobs
- knowledge of child development
- better relationships with children
- better contact with schools
- increased confidence/esteem.

What do you think the benefits of family learning might be for your child(ren)?

Prompts
- accelerated development, e.g. pre-school oral skills
- improved existing skills, e.g. in literacy and numeracy
- increased confidence/esteem
- improved health
- improved behaviour – positive attitudes
- pleasure in learning – normal adult activity too.

What do you think the benefits of family learning might be for others?

Prompts
- your family – improved relationships, better support, better communication
- your community – improved relationships, better support, better communication.

What about an organised family learning programme would make it successful?

Prompts
- location
- timing
- frequency
- overall duration
- members of own family present
- other participants (age groups, numbers, roles)
- provider(s) (multi-agency collaboration?)
- subject matter
  - ➤ improving child's skills
  - ➤ improving parenting skills
  - ➤ improving own skills
- formality – open/closed/drop-in
- assessment methods (self-assessment, practical exercises, psychometric tests, other tests, referral)
- delivery mode – small groups, workbooks, ICT, combinations.

COSTS OF FAMILY LEARNING

Could there be any drawbacks to family learning:
- for you?
- for your child(ren)?
- for others?

What about an organised family learning programme would make it unsuccessful?

Prompts
- location
- timing
- frequency
- overall duration
- members of own family present
- other participants (age groups, numbers, roles)
- provider(s) (multi-agency collaboration?)
- subject matter
  - ➤ improving child's skills

➤ improving parenting skills
➤ improving own skills
• formality – open/closed/drop-in
• assessment methods (self-assessment, practical exercises, psychometric tests, other tests, referral)
• delivery mode – small groups, workbooks, ICT, combinations.

IMPORTANCE OF, AND PARTICIPATION IN, FAMILY LEARNING

Is family learning important to you? Why?

Would you like to take part in an organised family learning programme in the future? Why?

What has stopped/would stop you from getting involved in family learning?

Prompts
• attitudes of self/family/others
• location/access
• time/timing
• commitment to frequency/duration
• other participants (age groups, numbers, roles)
• providers
• formality
• subject matter of courses on offer
• assessment methods
• delivery mode.

How could people be encouraged to participate in family learning programmes?
• men
• ethnic minorities
• most disadvantaged/poorest skilled families.

CLOSING COMMENTS

Is there anything you would like to add about your feelings concerning family learning?

Is there anything else you would like to say in relation to the things we have been discussing?

Bibliography

Alexander, T. and Clyne, P. (1995), *Riches Beyond Price: Making the most of family learning*. Leicester: NIACE.

Basic Skills Agency (1998), *Family Numeracy Adds Up*. London: Basic Skills Agency.

Bastiani, J. (1999), *SHARE: An evaluation of the first two years*. Coventry: CEDC.

Brooks, G., Gorman, T., Harman, J., Hutchison, D., Kendall, S. and Wilkin, A. (1999), *Family Literacy for New Groups*. London: Basic Skills Agency.

Brooks, G., Gorman, T., Harman, J., Hutchison, D. and Wilkin, A. (1996), *Family Literacy Works*. London: Basic Skills Agency.

Brooks, G., Harman, J., Hutchison, D., Wilkin, A. and Kinder, K. (1997), *Family Literacy Lasts*. London: Basic Skills Agency.

Buffton, J. (1999), *Family Learning: Taking the work forward*. Working paper. Second Report of the National Advisory Group for Continuing Education and Lifelong Learning. Online. Available HTTP:

<http://www.lifelonglearning.co.uk/nagcell2/wp-fam.pdf> (accessed 8 May 2003).

Bynner, J., Joshi, H. and Tsatsas, M. (1999), *Obstacles and Opportunities on the Route to Adulthood: Evidence from urban and rural Britain*. London: Smith Institute.

Bynner, J. and Steedman, J. (1995), *Difficulties with Adult Basic Skills*. London: Basic Skills Agency.

Campaign for Learning (2001), 'Why Family Learning?' *Journal of Lifelong Learning Initiatives*, 21, 8–10.

Campaign for Learning, NIACE, CEDC, Scottish Council Foundation and Education Extra (2000), *A Manifesto for Family Learning*. London: Campaign for Learning.

Community Education Development Centre (2001), *It's a Man Thing! Evaluation report of CEDC's Fathers and Reading Project*. Coventry: CEDC.

Cuckle, P. (1996), 'Children Learning to Read – Exploring home and school relationships'. *British Educational Research Journal*, 22, 17–32.

Department for Education and Employment (1999), *Learning to Succeed: Post-16 funding*. Second Technical Consultation Paper. London: The Stationery Office.

— (2000), *Skills for Life: The National Strategy for Improving Adult Literacy and Numeracy Skills*. A statement by the Hon. David Blunkett MP. London: DfEE.

Edwards, A. and Warin, J. (1999), 'Parental Involvement in Raising Pupils' Achievement in Primary Schools: Why bother?' *Oxford Review of Education*, 25, 325–41.

Flouri, E. and Buchanan, A. (2003), 'The Role of Father Involvement in Children's Later Mental Health'. *Journal of Adolescence*, 26 (1), 63–78.

Goleman, D. (1996), *Emotional Intelligence: Why it can matter more than IQ*. London: Bloomsbury.

Gorard, S., Rees, G., Renold, E. and Fevre, R. (1998), *Family Influences on Participation in Lifelong Learning*. Working Paper 15. Cardiff: Cardiff University.

Haggart, J. (2000), *Learning Legacies: A guide to family learning*. Leicester: NIACE.

— (2001), *Walking Ten Feet Tall: A Toolkit for Family Learning Practitioners*. London: DfES and NIACE.

Henricson, C., Katz, I., Mesie, J., Sandison, M. and Tunstill, J. (2001), *National Mapping of Family Services in England and Wales – A consultation document*. London: National Family and Parenting Institute.

Lewis, A. (2000), *SHARE at Key Stage 2: Pilot project 1999*. Evaluation Report. Coventry: CEDC.

McDonald, L., Billingham, S., Conrad, T., Morgan, A. and Payton, E. (1997), 'Families and Schools Together (FAST), Integrating community development with clinical strategies'. *Families in Society – The Journal of Contemporary Human Services*, 78, 140–155.

Moore, M. and Wade, B. (1998), *Bookstart: The first five years. A description and evaluation of an exploratory British project to encourage sharing books with babies*. London: Book Trust.

Mortimore, P. (1988), *School Matters: The junior years*. Wells: Open Books.

Office for Standards in Education (2000), *Family Learning: A survey of current practice*. London: Ofsted. Also online. Available HTTP: <http://www.ofsted.gov.uk/publications/docs/465.pdf> (accessed 8 May 2003).

Osborne, A. F. (1990), 'Resilient Children: A longitudinal study of high-achieving socially disadvantaged children'. *Early Childhood Development and Care*, 62, 23–47.

Parsons, S. and Bynner, J. (1998), *Influences on Adult Basic Skills*. London: Basic Skills Agency.

Roberts, E., Bornstein, M.H., Slater, A.M. and Barrett, J. (1999), 'Early Cognitive Development and Parental Education'. *Infant and Child Development*, 8, 131–40.

Smith, J. and Spurling, A. (2000), 'Motivation for developmental learning: the individual and the family'. Paper presented at the Campaign for Learning workshop Motivation for Developmental Learning: The individual and the family, London, September.

Tizard, B., Blatchford, P., Burke, J., Farquhar, C. and Plewis, I. (1988), *Young Children at School in the Inner Cities*. London: Lawrence Erlbaum Associates.